OUT OF THE STORM - A COP'S JOURNEY

A VETERAN POLICE OFFICER'S JOURNEY TO HELL AND BACK

COLIN DIXON

OUT OF THE STORM - A COP'S JOURNEY

A VETERAN POLICE OFFICER'S JOURNEY TO HELL AND BACK

COLIN DIXON with PATRICIA SUTCLIFFE

OUT OF THE STORM - A COP'S JOURNEY

COPYRIGHT © 2021 COLIN DIXON

All rights reserved

IBSN-9798761465046

Some names and details in this book have been changed to protect anonymity

COLIN DIXON

DEDICATION

I dedicate this book to:

Sarah Dixon (my wife)
Junior (our beloved dog)
Nathan Dixon (my son)
Harry Beeby (my grandfather)
Ronald & Florence (my parents)
Jean & David (my in-laws)
Carole (sister)

'Thank you all for believing in me'

ACKNOWLEDGMENTS

Patricia Sutcliffe
www.patriciasutcliffeauthor.com)
For making this possible.
John Gee, Paul Hannaford, Paul Harkin,
Sarah and Nathan Dixon
For their valued contributions to this book.

The following Police Officers
Tony Rushman (RIP), Darren 'Tez' Simpson RIP),
Dave Gross and Sabre, Paul Money, Barry
Aveyard, Dave Matthews, Paul Cooper, Andy Firth,
Andy Webster, Imran Razak, Mark Shaw, Dean O'Kell,
Dean Turner, Paul Stockwell, Joe Dainton, Ben
Sweeney, Johan Neethling, Dave Laybourne (RIP),
Mark Hunter, Dickie Whitehead

The following Civilians
Max Troisi, Alan Parkinson, Dr James Hirst
For their support and friendship. It means so much
to me.

FOREWORD by Patricia Sutcliffe

COLIN DIXON

'Out of the Storm, A Cop's Journey' recounts a veteran police officer's 30 years in the force. His story is raw, the incidents real, the danger overwhelming. This is a tale of dedication and loyalty in the face of adversity. From his early days as a young and naïve rookie cop pounding the streets, then moving into the dark world of addiction as an experienced member of a Drugs Enforcement Team. Colin Dixon has seen it all. His journey on the front line is told with the same passion he gave to his job. His stories, full of courage, show the strength needed to be the highly commended officer he became. Colin's journey guides the reader through the streets of West Yorkshire and the constant fight against crime. From drug dens to high-speed road pursuits. From internal politics and betrayal to the dark days of pain and destruction. Out of the Storm, a Cop's Journey has it all. Without doubt, Colin Dixon suffered for his work, but he also found the true meaning of forgiveness, turning the isolation he felt into hope. It is said that the devil is in the detail and this book holds nothing back.

Theodore Roosevelt

It's not the critic who counts, nor the person who points out where the strong man stumbles, or where the doer of deeds could have done better. The credit belongs to the man who is actually in the arena, whose face is marred by dust and sweat and blood, who knows great devotion and enthusiasm, and whom, if he fails, at least fails whilst attempting daringly so that his place shall never be with those odd and timid souls who know neither victory nor defeat. You've never lived until you've almost died, for those that have had to fight for it, life truly has a flavour the protected shall never know.

COLIN DIXON

JUNIOR (RIP)
Always by my side

Chapter 1–A Steep Learning Curve

Once you stop learning, you start dying
Albert Einstein

I hear so many times from police officers who say it was their dream to go into the Force. I can't say that. I didn't have a dream; I didn't think I would become a veteran of 30 years. It was a feeling inside of me that policing could be something that I would be suited to, as simple as that. There was no yearning. I didn't have an epiphany.

Was I naïve about what to expect? Of course, I was. I wasn't worried about the change in lifestyle. I was a steady lad anyhow. I had a job in management, so was a dedicated person. I didn't go out drinking much or nightclubbing like many of my age, so had no reservations about losing "friends" if I joined the police. I suppose I always wanted to make something of myself, and it prepared me to put in the work of achieving that.

I was outgoing and no shrinking violet, so I was quietly confident that I could do well as a police officer. I felt I knew a bit about life, limited as it may have been, so the restrictions associated with being an officer wouldn't really affect my lifestyle. The only problem I could see was that I hadn't done particularly well at school; I had no qualifications; I hadn't put the effort into my academic subjects, so when I discovered I had to take a basic entrance test; I was apprehensive. I relied on my wonderful mum to help me by giving me tips on English and Maths. I got 107, and I needed 100 or more marks to get through. I passed. Thanks, mum. I owe you so much for everything in life that you did for me.

OUT OF THE STORM - A COP'S JOURNEY

In the early 90s, there were no computer systems like there are now. Training was analysing scenarios and learning legislation, which took some doing. The thing that still stands out to me is the amount of drill work we did. I'm not very coordinated, so wasn't particularly keen on learning to march, morning, noon and night. I just didn't see the benefit to me. It consumed a lot of time, up and down on the parade ground. I just wanted to get on with the actual police work.

With time, I realised that the purpose of it was to form a camaraderie, a bonding amongst the recruits, but I still preferred the practical side of training. The side I knew I would need once doing the job. The training was quite physical, but I had expected that. A lot of cross-country running, exercising in the gym, self-defence and everything I thought would be in there. I really enjoyed my training. I knew I was getting fitter and more knowledgeable by the day. More than ready to take up my role as a fully-fledged police officer.

Yes, there were a few trainers who were a little overzealous. If you got something wrong in your practice pocketbook, even a line not straight enough, they would make a big thing of it. Every cop goes through training and takes away what they want from it. It's like any form of education, the learning in a classroom differs from the hands-on reality of the job. I just see it as they put the foundations down and it's up to you to build on them.

My first posting was at Garforth in the East Leeds area. It was a good start for me. I really enjoyed it there because it was a combination of rural areas, like Ledston, Ledsham and Kippax, combined with urban areas such as Leeds 15 with its big council estates that included Swarcliffe and Whinmoor. It gave me an excellent grounding because of the need for different policing methods.

There was a bit of what some would see as bullying today at the Station. They would take the mick out of my Northeast accent. They would expect me to make tea every day, silly stuff really, but I was the new recruit, and I expected it. I loved it there; I have to say. It was hard work. We did seven nights shifts in a row. After seven-night shifts, I would finish at 6am on the

Monday morning and be back on at 2pm on Wednesday. When not on night shifts for three weeks, we had quick changeovers where you finished at 10pm and had to be back on duty at 6am the next day. Add to that your travelling time and you were lucky to get five hours of sleep in between shifts. It was much harder compared with shifts today, but I was much younger so could take it in my stride then.

I was lucky; I got a former CID officer as my tutor who had been put back into uniform as a punishment for a misdemeanor. I benefited from his demotion. He proved to be a real rough diamond but was very experienced and had gained a lot of knowledge in his 20 years' service. One thing he taught me which I'll never forget was the 'Devil is always in the Detail.' I'll explain more about the importance of that in a later chapter.

So, my probation period started and with it my steep learning curve. I remember on one occasion when I was a year into the job; I discovered how evil someone could really be. It started when two well-known criminals who were also brothers had a confrontation with another police officer. They held him hostage and repeatedly threatened to kill him by sliding a knife across his throat. Physically, the officer survived, but mentally he was extremely traumatised and suffered from what they would diagnose today as PTSD.

I can recall the time when I encountered one of the two brothers; it was a dark winter's night, and I was with a more experienced officer. We spotted a car that we knew belonged to them, which was parked up outside a pub. Although we hadn't been present at the initial incident, we both knew what they had done to the officer. We waited 30 minutes, then one brother came out of the pub and staggered into the car and drove off. We followed him. We were in a plain car that didn't have blue lights or sirens; so, we asked for a marked Police car to assist in stopping him. Before this could happen, the vehicle pulled into a petrol station. He got out of the car and started filling it up with petrol. I approached him. The stench of alcohol on his breath was strong. I told him I required a breath test as I suspected him of drink driving.

He totally ignored me and continued to put petrol in the car. I told him to stop. I again requested he take a breath test. He played dumb and refused to comply with my request. It was at this point I arrested him for failing to provide a roadside breath test. Close up, I could really feel the evil presence of this man. I knew we were in for a terrific battle. What I didn't know was this arrest was going to be the most violent and impactive one in my career to date.

He used extreme force to resist being arrested. It took my partner and me all of our combined strength to get him to the ground. He became like a wildcat. This lasted several minutes, but it felt much longer. There were times I thought we wouldn't be able to keep hold of him. The strength and determination he had were unbelievable. He came very close to overpowering us.

I can see it now vividly. We were both on top of him, frantically trying to handcuff him. He was shouting and screaming obscenities at us. In between this mayhem, I think my partner had pressed the panic button on his radio, urgently requesting other units to attend. Adrenaline was racing through me, my heart pumping furiously. I feared that if he had a knife or weapon hidden on him, and he could get to it, he would use it on us both with no hesitation.

Finally, we got one handcuff on him, but because he struggled so violently; it was hard to get the other cuff on, leaving his other hand free. He then reached up and gripped my face with his nails and tried to gouge my right eye out. It was by the Grace of God that his grip was just over my eye. A few centimeters lower, I could now be blind. My face dripped with blood where he had gouged his fingernails into me.

It was such a relief when we got both handcuffs on him. It was then I felt my shirt was wet; I thought it was blood, but thankfully it was just sweat. It drenched me from the pure exertion of the struggle. Other officers arrived a short time later, but he continued to be just as aggressive and violent, repeatedly threatening our lives and screaming how he wished my mum would die of cancer.

Never had I seen such hatred and venom in a person. When we got him to the custody area at the police station, it took several officers to restrain him before it was safe to release his handcuffs. He was subsequently charged, then bailed for assault on my partner and me and for failing to give a roadside breath test. He didn't bother to turn up for the court hearing, so the Magistrates issued a warrant for his arrest.

Local searches for him proved fruitless. Then I received some intelligence that he had fled to Ireland. I put an alert on any crossings from Ireland, so I would be notified if he tried to cross the border back into England. Sure enough, 18 months later, I was contacted by the Garda, the police of Southern Ireland. They informed me he had left Ireland and was travelling to Leeds. They gave me his forwarding address.

I knew I had to act quickly, so I sought assistance from colleagues that included a dog handler and his police dog. After a quick briefing, we went to the address and surrounded it before knocking on the front door. It turned out to be a B & B, and we saw the suspect in an upstairs bedroom. Cautiously, we entered the property and found him. This time he offered no physical violence, but the look he gave me was the evilest look I had ever seen; it was clear he knew I was the person who had arrested him at the petrol station. I cautioned him and arrested him for failure to attend court. He didn't reply but looked straight through me. The presence of eight police officers and a dog in the house may have quelled his violence, but the sickening silence he maintained on his way to the police station was menacing. The way he stared at me, malevolent.

Months passed before he went to Crown Court for his trail. As I stood in the box to give evidence, I felt his eyes burning into me, but I continued, refusing to let him intimidate me. My partner and a civilian witness corroborated my evidence. The case lasted a few days until at last; the jury reached a decision.
'NOT GUILTY.'

Unbelievable! Not guilty, I'll never forget the incident. I could have been blinded, and they found him 'Not guilty.' At first, I struggled to believe the decision, then I saw him grinning at me. He continued to grin and stare as I left the court. Unwittingly, I had left my calling card with the evilest man I had met. I left court feeling totally deflated. Justice, as disappointing as it seemed to me, had been served.

He walked away that day, a free man. I walked away, a changed man. From that day on, I became more aware of my surroundings. My observations heightened. I would know if someone was watching me as I started or finished my shifts. Why? Because my sixth sense told me this story wasn't over with.

Some years had passed when I found out he had joined one of the Hell's Angel motorcycle gangs and was committing some horrific, violent acts against his victims. As part of his initiation to join the gang, he had to walk into a pub and smash a hammer across the head of an innocent customer. It didn't surprise me he was prepared to do this with no hesitation.

These gang members were very evil, involved in widespread drug dealing, extortion, and sickening violence every day. One of their victims had a machete put into his mouth to extort money from him. Another had his hair shaved off and his head repeatedly ducked under water. So violent were the gang that one of their members, unable to tolerate the violence any longer, attempted to leave. His punishment, hours of torture before repeatedly being stabbed 15 times and left for dead.

Learning about these acts it relieved me I was no longer involved in any investigation with him. Months of mayhem continued to be created by the gang, leading to a massive police operation, which saw them all being arrested and remanded to jail. The relief was short-lived when midway through the trial; I got a call from a solicitor asking for me by name. I asked who he was and the minute he told me he was working for a barrister acting on behalf of him, the hairs on the back of my neck went up. I had a feeling of dread.

The solicitor told me they required me at the trial. They made the request as his client was claiming past police corruption, and he was using the failure of my previous trial against him as evidence of this claim. He clearly hadn't forgotten my dealings with him, even though several years had now passed. Legal wrangling between the barristers ensued until eventually they satisfied the Judge there had been no dishonesty or corruption in my investigation.

Relieved, I was told they didn't require me, but the greatest relief came when he and his gang received substantial prison sentences.

There's a saying that every contact leaves a trace. Locard's principle says that the perpetrator of a crime will bring something into the crime scene and leave with something from it. This is equally true with human contact with one another. Such contacts in your years of policing can certainly alter the way you view society. You are constantly dealing with both the perpetrators and victims of crimes; you are experiencing the darker side of human nature and its negative effect on others. Frequently witnessing inadequate and disappointing sentences and then having to deliver this news to the victims can make your perspective on society very negative. Is it any wonder that many officers become cynical and disillusioned?

Training school taught us self-defence, issued us with protective gear, but they never taught us about any possible effects on our mental health and how to recognise them, or how we should deal with it. It took me a while to come to terms with the judicial system and recognise that it wasn't personal; it was just the way it worked. I may not like it, but I knew I must accept it, otherwise I would become very bitter and twisted.

Over the years, I realised that there were hard men in every area we policed. In one village, there was a man who saw himself as the resident tough nut. He took it upon himself to show how much he detested the local constabulary. His contact with the police was always hostile. It came as no surprise then when I heard that South Yorkshire Police wanted him for questioning about a suspected burglary.

Once a person is circulated as wanted, we will be on the lookout for them until we have arrested them. A short while after they had circulated the suspect, my partner and I had seen him and chased him on foot, but he evaded us, despite having Dave, a dog handler, and his faithful dog Sabre, assisting us. Evading us was a genuine achievement in the eyes of the hard man.

But, as they say, every dog has his day. Sabre's came quickly. It was a week later, on a dark winter's night. I was on patrol, nearing the end of my shift. We spotted a car slowly pulling out from a cul-de-sac. It was being driven by the wanted man's brother, another well-known criminal. I saw a dark shadow get out of the vehicles passenger seat and start running in the opposite direction to us. Instinctively, I knew something wasn't right, so added two and two together and it made four. I was sure that the figure was the wanted man.

I gave chase, and he sprinted away, disappearing into a network of gardens, residential houses and backstreets. Spitting feathers, I was just about to give up when I decided on one last ditched attempt at getting him. Knowing how close we had previously got using a police dog, I radioed in to see if there was a dog patrol in the area. I was in luck; X Ray Delta 88 was nearby. It thrilled me when I saw it was Dave and Sabre on duty, and available to assist us.

I showed Dave the last place I had seen the suspect, and he placed a tracking harness on Sabre. Immediately, the dog got to work. With his nose to the ground, he tracked the wanted man to a nearby house. There we faced a man who answered the door. He looked guilty and fumbled with his words, saying nobody other than himself was in the house.

We explained our suspicions that a wanted male was in the house, and he allowed us entry into it. We found the suspect in an upstairs bedroom. I cautioned him and told him he was under arrest on suspicion of burglary.

'I'm not fucking coming.' Was his immediate response.

We tried to talk to him and make him see reason, but he grabbed a small object from the floor and threatened to harm himself if we got near him. I couldn't tell what he was holding. It was small, and I had to make an assessment. Whatever he was holding, it could easily have been a weapon. I knew my partner and I could probably overcome the man but not sure of what he had in his hand; I was taking no risks.

I requested the services of Dave and Sabre, who were waiting outside. As they came up the stairs, I quickly moved aside. The last thing I wanted was to get bitten. Now they were in charge of the standoff and a few feet from the suspect. He was told to drop the item in his hand and comply with being arrested. I'm now thinking that the man would come to his senses, but no. Even the sight of an angry dog straining at the leash and ready to attack didn't deter him.

'Fuck off! I've told you I'm not coming. I'll put this in your face if you come near me.' he shouted, indicating to the article in his hand.

Wrong reply! In an instance, Sabre was released. He moved in like an Exocet missile and a flash of teeth later; he had inflicted several bites on the man's legs, who was now writhing in agony on the floor. The item he had been holding turned out to be a toy airplane.

His injuries were so bad he couldn't walk, so we had to fire lift him out of the house to our police car. They say dogs can't smile, but I could have sworn Sabre smiled at me as he jumped into his police van. After the arrest, we would normally take him into custody, but his legs were so badly injured that we bypassed this, taking him straight to hospital. I spent the next few hours pushing him around in a wheelchair. Once able, we passed him to South Yorkshire Police for further investigation into the burglary offence.

A week later, he was visited by officers about an unrelated incident. They found him laid on his settee, crutches by his side, obviously still in a great deal of pain. Puss was oozing from the bandages wrapped around his legs. There he remained whilst the officer conducted his enquiry. His parting shot to the cop as he left.

'You can tell that dog officer I'm going to kill his dog when I'm better.'

To date, Sabre is still awaiting the rematch.

Chapter 2 - On the Beat

'It's the repetition of affirmations that leads to belief, once that belief becomes conviction, things really start to happen'

After my probation years were over, I felt like a real cop. I had so much more knowledge than when I had started; I felt capable of dealing with most day-to-day incidents and was ready to be out on my own. I had spent a lot of my early days out on foot patrol, and I enjoyed those days.

Killingbeck Police station is where I did three years on the drugs team. What a revelation that was to me. I was seeing things with heroin and addictions that I didn't know existed. What a learning curve it proved to be. From a beat cop to a drugs team officer, the difference is startling. A real eye opener. I never knew such hopelessness and despair existed in some sections of society.

Without doubt, being a police officer changes your perception of the world. You are predominately dealing with criminals who care little for others or their possessions, and then you have to deal with the victims traumatised by the crimes they have suffered. You know the pain they feel when the suspect gets off with a non-custodial sentence, such as community service or a small fine. Nothing can be done, but I used to feel extremely disappointed, as did the victims.

As a police officer, you must learn to accept that you can't change the judicial system and the outcomes, as difficult as that is sometimes. Managing the victim's expectations and your own emotions were key to maintaining a healthy mind set and mental wellbeing.

One of the worst cases I ever remember and which affected me greatly was when my partner and I were called out to a road traffic accident in Allerton Bywater. A car had gone into an adverse camber on a bend, lost control, and hit a lamppost. The passenger had got out with minor injuries, but the driver was still in the car, which was now wedged up against the lamppost. When we arrived at the scene, the fire brigade was already there. I saw one of the brigade lads crying. I thought,

'what's he crying for?' What have I missed? There were no cuts or blood evident on the driver's face or body. I thought he was still alive, but just unconscious. When we pulled him out of the car, his body was limp, and it became obvious he was dead. The impact of the accident had resulted in a broken neck. Dead at seventeen years old.

My partner and I had to drive a few miles to his home address to break the devastating news to his family. I knocked on the front door and saw a silhouette coming towards me. All I can think of as I see the figure moving towards the door is that I'm about to destroy your lives forever. These were the last few seconds of peace they would have. The boy's mum answered the door, and I knew I had to tell her the tragic news: her son was dead. I didn't want to do this, but it was my job and I had to stay strong and professional.

I walked into the living room and was just about to deliver what we call in the job a death warning. I started "Your son" but then, for a second, I was distracted by what I saw on the mantlepiece. It was a 'congratulations on passing your driving test' card. The lad had just passed his test the day before. It took me totally off guard. I still delivered the message. I had to watch as his mum became hysterical. As if this wasn't enough for a parent to bear, we had to take her to the undertakers to identify her son's lifeless body. Throughout this hellish journey, her grief was heart-breaking and overwhelming.

You knew that here was a mother who yesterday was celebrating with her son the passing of his driving test. Today she is mourning his death. His future wiped out and his parents' hopes and aspirations for him demolished.

As police officers, we live in a world of angst, predominately it's all you experience. Criminals have little, if any, respect for their victims who have to live with the consequences of becoming a crime statistic. When I first started my policing career, I genuinely thought I could make a big difference, but soon found out I couldn't. I could only make a slight difference, and it took me a good number of years to come to terms with this. As someone who is passionate about their work, I found that difficult to accept. I had always thought that hard work, dedication and enthusiasm would equate to success. How wrong I was.

Why? Because we are dealing with a force that is unstoppable. Some criminals today are made of a different cloth. They think it's their right to take what they want, when they want, and consequences don't come into it. They aren't there to pick up the aftermath of their crimes and rarely see or care about the mental damage and upset caused to their victims.

The number of times I've had to tell a parent that their son or daughter is a drug addict. They break down in disbelief. Mortified that we have arrested their child for possession of drugs, and we are now searching their house. We have an Inspector's authority to search, and we are in the privacy of their home. Their first reaction will be, 'what are you here for? Is it John, is he okay?' We tell them it's a drug related investigation. Their mouths fall open, it's the first they have heard or known of drugs. It can't be true, not their child. Sadly, it is true, and it horrifies them.

To leave them with the news that their loved one is addicted to drugs is life changing. Often, they cannot understand how the child that they thought they knew so well, has managed to hide a side of their lives from them. They have seen no obvious signs, but they weren't looking either. Why would they be? Only if the addiction is out of control do they notice the physical changes in appearances or the negative lifestyle choices they have made.

If it involves heroin, it's likely they've been taking it for some time, but there are some addicts who can take it and still function from day to day. From my experience most addicts love and care for their parents, however, when addicted to heroin or other highly addictive drugs, that love is tested to its limits and beyond. The addict becomes a different person to the one previously known by their families.

Police officers can usually assess a situation quickly because of an enhanced sixth sense that develops when you are repeatedly dealing with difficult and conflicting situations where people don't always tell you the truth. If you can spot it earlier, you can be ready for it. An example is when you are called to a violent domestic dispute, you enter the house, and you are immediately looking for tell-tale signs in order to establish where the likely threat of violence will come from.

I liken it to a snake, if you grab hold of it properly the first time; you stop it biting. If you fumble or lose your grip because you've not seen the warning signs and someone is extremely violent, then that's when you're going to get badly bitten. At that moment, you have lost control of the situation and the situation is controlling you. If you aren't aware of what can happen and aren't looking for it, you are effectively endangering yourself, your colleagues, and perhaps members of the public.

Imagine, you are in someone's house whereas far as they are concerned; they are the king of their castle. To them, you have no authority or right to be in there unless you have a warrant (with domestic incidents, this is rarely the case). They tell you to get out and their frightened partner tells you they don't want to complain or press charges. However, in domestic abuse cases, the suspects are often arrested at the scene to prevent further violence and sometimes victimless prosecutions can be pursued when the victim refuses to make a statement. To the suspect, it's a genuine injustice, so it's fair game in their minds for them to lash out at you and resist being arrested.

There was one domestic incident where we had to go into a crime scene as a deranged father had stabbed his two children to death. We were wearing masks to protect the scene, but the odour of death was strong in the air. The father had been arrested, and the children's bodies removed, but the bedsheets were still blood stained. It was a dreadful scene to attend but knowing it has involved children makes it even more gut wrenching. You are talking about teenage children with all of their lives in front of them, taken away by a person they look to as their protector, their father.

It's a murder scene. We had to do a fingertip search and knowing the atrocity that has taken place obviously steers your emotions. You are invading their personal space, going into every nook and cranny. It's the last place these children were alive, and you are in it. You look around the room, see the type of lives they led, the things they held as precious. Photographs of happy times, all now tinged with death. I wished I wasn't there, but knew I had to be. That makes you stay and do your job. You don't forget the smell; it stays with you for a long time, and perhaps forever. What started as a domestic dispute has ended in a fatal tragedy.

The job requires us to attend many violent domestics where we are in danger of being assaulted. I recall one where a female colleague was badly assaulted. My sixth sense kicked in before we got to the house. The female victim had called 999 to say there had been an incident involving her partner. As we pulled up at the house, something told me this would not be straightforward.

I saw a woman walking up the path towards the house where we had received the call from, and I remember asking her if she still needed us as we were late in getting there because of a busy night shift. The woman said, 'I think so, I think he's still in the house, he's been there most of the night, but I've just taken my kid to school.' We all entered the house. The woman isn't complaining of any assault, and she has no visible injuries. She wants her partner removing from her home. He's there, acting menacingly, but he doesn't live there, so I give him the option to leave. He tells me he is not leaving, so all I can do is tell him if he doesn't, I will arrest him.

He's very arrogant and sure of himself and tells me that if he has to leave, he will just stand on the corner outside of the property until we go and then he will return. Under these circumstances, I had no choice but to arrest him for a breach of the peace. He lets me handcuff him to the front but as we go to leave the house; he seizes his moment. I'm walking him out, holding his handcuffs. I'm leading him from the front and my partner is behind us. He then kicks me as hard as he can to the side of my right knee.

I immediately drop to the floor with the force of his boot smashing into my kneecap. He then swings around, using the handcuffs, he then smashes the female officer in the face with them. He's raging and dangerous. I get back up from the floor and can hear the screams of my partner. I'm thinking, 'shit, this is bad'. I know I must regain control of the situation.

Everything is in slow motion then; his face is red with anger, and he is very threatening. I spray him in the face with the CS gas I carry. It doesn't affect him at all; it doesn't on some people. He's now goading me. 'Is that all you've got? I'm gonna kill you.' I've a colleague still on the ground, badly hurt. I must then use my baton and some extreme force to get him under control. His partner is screaming for me to stop.

At the time I am thinking, you are joking; you called us out. Understanding domestic abuse much more now, I totally understand why the victim said that. Her fear was that when he gets out of police custody, she will pay for his arrest as she was the one that called us. She knows she will live in fear throughout whatever sentence he gets for assaulting a police officer, waiting for the day he returns. The incident ended with him being subdued, but only after some extreme force. She was right to fear him. Although he was a convicted criminal; he didn't get a custodial sentence for the assaults on us that day.

So, an officer is kicked hard, and another brutally attacked and badly injured, and he gets fined and a non-custodial punishment. When this happens, you can't help thinking, 'what am I doing here? There is no law and order.' It all seems pointless and can be very demoralising. When officers become victims of violent attacks whilst doing their duty, there must be some consequences, surely? The criminal will argue about their rights, but what about the rights of their victims?

We see so many injustices for the public and officers alike that over time, you become desensitised to it. I think I am one of the last of a generation of foot beat officers. Car patrols have taken over, losing a lot of direct contact with the public. I don't think there will be many cops in the future who can say, 'I've done 30 years on the front line.'

The way things are now, the pace of the job and increasing violence on the streets, I predict that many new recruits will join, stay seven or eight years and leave with a good C.V. and of course with the mandatory degree officers now have to obtain during their training.

There are times I sit and think about what has changed since my start date in the 90s compared to today, and why? The more I ponder over this, the more I realise that there is no one answer. There are several layers of reasons. Criminals have never really liked the police, but there was still some respect. This is now mostly extinct, along with the extended family role. There was a time when you knew if you got in trouble with the police, you would be in more trouble from your own parents and then from your grandparents.

People in general had a belief system; morals were important, as was knowing right from wrong. We didn't have social media platforms spreading detailed information about how to get away with crimes or showing toxic videos of assaults on innocent individuals and police officers. The role of media and how it reports incidents have played a large part in the way the public perceives the police.

We have become a society of have's and have not's and whilst that hasn't changed, the reporting of it has. We have stories of Government corruption and wrongdoing giving criminals an attitude of, 'If it's okay for them, it's okay for us.' This has all made the job of a police officer harder.

Another key factor is rising crime rates. In the early 90s, the number of calls received by the police was relatively low compared with today. Their workload now overwhelms officers not just with the call handling but with the amount of IT work that accompanies any arrest or call out to an incident and the subsequent investigation.

In the 90s, 70 percent of the job was doing it, 30 percent was written reports. Now the monster of IT has reversed that statistic. We often spend more time at a computer inputting and duplicating information than being out on the streets dealing with crime. Yes, computers have brought many benefits to the police force, but they have also taken away a lot of self-generated work and positive interaction with communities and residents.

Today's police officers are being worn out and often overwhelmed with the workload. The job for life philosophy has now changed. When I started, I was dealing with a different beast than the one found today. What I envisaged the job to be wasn't too far away from what I found it to be. The one to one on the streets, the learning, doing the job, getting it all off to a fine art. Now, it's more like the fire brigade going from one call to another with a brief respite in between. You must become hardened quickly or you will go under.

I think there is another side to the number of reports, and IT involved in the job. At one time, there was a great camaraderie in the office. You had time to pass the day, share a joke or two, but now, there are hundreds of emails, reports and calls to deal with and the social side has become restricted. You are often locked away on a computer; it detracts from the quality of engagement with people. You must concentrate on a screen and there is less time to bond with others. It can be very insular.

There was an officer. I can see him now. He was an older guy coming towards the end of his service, about 55 years old. He was struggling with the first computer system we inherited in the 90s, and someone was showing him something quite basic on it that even I knew. I felt sorry for him. I thought of all the years of experience he had, and now his Achilles heel was a simple computer. Fast forward 28 years later to Halifax and I was now that man.

In 2008, a new system from Canada had come in. NicheRMS, a full-featured police records management system. Designed to be used by multiple police forces. The system is excellent and has many benefits, but for me, it's also complicated. I got into it; I had to, but I found it extremely complex.

I'll tell you more about it when I relate stories of my time at Halifax.

I remember a time when I was on the Regional Roads Crime Team; it was 2009. This was my first specialist role, and it was a new venture that involved four neighbouring police forces working together. Our role was to target organised criminals who crossed police borders and used their vehicles to commit crimes. It included large-scale drug dealing and money laundering. They provided us with high performance vehicles. Training included an intense four-week advanced driver's course and a tactical pursuit and containment course, (this is where you learn to box in suspects vehicles, usually at high speeds). Commonly known as TPAC.

There I was doing what I had joined the police to do, looking for criminals and having the time to do this. After I had made an arrest, I was in the privileged position of being able to hand the prisoner over to whichever Force or Police Division I had made the arrest in. We left other officers with the time consuming casework and further enquiries. I wasn't doing any of the redactions on court files or the sometimes complex further investigations. We were doing some 'exciting policing'. We could well argue that what we did was the straightforward part. We were out on the roads in fast motors doing what most cops want to do, catching criminals.

I feel for today's front-line officers, day after day, dealing with all the calls we give them that no one else wants, the domestics, the drunks, the fights and everything else. They have one of the most difficult roles in the police. They get little recognition. They are just pushed and pushed. There is no end to it. When you are younger, you can cope with the pace of front-line duty, but as you get older, you slow down. You feel worn out by it and as you reach your 50s; it becomes harder to overpower and catch the younger criminals on today's streets.

Before I move too far ahead, however, I will say that I had some of my biggest laughs as a rookie cop. You are the new boy; you are the target of jokes and jibes. There was this one lad called Tez, unbeknown to him they had put an L plate on the back of his police jacket and allowed him to do a few hours foot beat around Garforth until a member of the public took pity on him and alerted him to his new "badge" They were always looking to catch the probationers out, but I thought I was too smart for that.

Well, I wasn't. One time they sent me to a report of a sudden death, or so I thought. I knocked on the door of this property. It didn't look like a normal type of premise, but as I looked around; I realised they had sent me to an undertaker. There was always stuff like that going on.

Chapter 3-Developing Awareness

'Self-awareness doesn't stop you from making mistakes. It allows you to learn from them'

Over time officers develop a sixth sense, it's like an energy. You feel it when dealing with some people. I still possess some of that today despite being retired, although not as much as when I was doing the job. Recently I was walking through Wakefield city centre, and I nearly bumped into a lad on a push bike at the top of an alleyway. I looked at him and he looked at me, well; he looked straight through me before riding off. His eyes said everything. They were cold and vicious. It was that look. You can't touch it, but you can feel it.

As I left the alley to go onto the main street, there was a beggar. Sat there, he looked at me with totally different eyes, which told me he was a probably a decent man but down on his luck. You can tell a lot from the way people look at you. They say the eyes are the window to the soul and I totally agree with that. It's an important skill for a police officer to have.

There's no shame in feeling fear, it's what you do with it that counts. I have no reservations in telling you that frequently in my police career; I felt a great deal of fear prior to having to arrest certain suspects. I developed a good sense for when things were going to be tricky.

As a police officer, you are often viewed differently. Some people are respectful and courteous, but others are confrontational, taking any chance they can to be abusive. There have been many incidents of officers suffering serious and often life changing injuries whilst attempting to make an arrest. In extreme circumstances, this can result in their deaths. This is the worst possible thing you fear. Some readers may remember Glen Goodman, a Special Constable in the 90s, and the Mad Dog McGregor incident.

This incident was horrific. North Yorkshire Police stop McGregor and another in a vehicle. They provide false personal details to the officers and when asked where they've been, they say a pub in Wetherby, but the pub they mention isn't in Wetherby. McGregor was wanted at the time for a murder in Ireland and realises that he's likely to be detained. Now he reveals his shocking true identity.

Out of nowhere, he produces a gun and fires at the police car. It hits the officer who was carrying out the roadside checks. A bullet passes through his radio and ricochets into his body. Thankfully, this radio saves him as the bullet is redirected from hitting his heart. Special Constable Goodman attempts to run to safety across the A64 and is shot in the back, dead.

A week later, I recall a time when I was dealing with a regular villain. When I had finished with him, he said under his breath, but loud enough for me to hear. 'You should have been that special that was shot.' Now I remember Glen Goodman when they put his picture in the paper, reporting he had been murdered. He was holding his baby boy. I looked at the photo. My son was about the same age. It hit me as I looked at them. That gut wrenching feeling inside my stomach. What would now happen to the officer's family and his young baby who was now without his father?

We don't know what is around the corner. Perhaps that's a good thing. Knowing a colleague has been killed in the line of duty has a devastating effect on every officer. To hear someone come out with such a statement makes you livid. He chose the wrong time to say that. I leant over to him and said, 'If I hear you say anything like that again, you'll be arrested like you've never been arrested before.' He said nothing else. If he had, there would have been consequences.

Ironically, that same week, I am on nights. I get to the fifth night of a seven-night stretch, and I arrest a drink driver. He's a young lad, but he's vile and incensed that I have caught him. He's probably done this several times before and for some unknown reason, he's got it in his head that I'm a Special Constable. Initially, I go along with it. Then he says. 'If I'd known you were a Special, I wouldn't have let you arrest me.' He's muttering on and we book him into custody. He doesn't provide two specimens of breath and elects to provide a urine sample. This results in us having to wait an hour for him to provide these samples.

I'm left on my own with him in the custody area and he's chipping away at me, chipping away for all he's worth. I ignore him. I will not let him get the better of me when he then says, "you should have been that special that was shot last week". I can't believe this and think I'm hearing things. I ask him to repeat what he said. I can feel the rage building up in me as he repeats, 'I said you should have been that fucking special that got shot last week.' He then shouts, "I'm not waiting here anymore" and attempts to get out of the custody area. I grab hold of him. I activate the alarm strip, which is on the wall and used in emergency situations. Within moments, other officers arrive, and I leave. I know I'm no longer the most suitable officer to deal with this man.

It just shows how someone saying the wrong words at the wrong time can affect you. Had I allowed my anger to get the better of me, I would have lost my job. When my Sergeant and other officers came in, I left them to sit with him. When you deal with people like that, you wonder what type of minds they have to come out with such loathsome comments. You ask yourself, why are they being so hateful and saying these things? You realise that their outlook on life and moral compass is so very different from yours. They lash out with anything to hurt or goad you, without thought, without rationale, with hatred. What kind of lives have they had to make them choose to behave this way?

Thankfully, not every suspect is the same and for the vast amount of my police career, I really enjoyed my time. My job was always varied, interesting, and I felt I was doing some good. Prior to joining the police, I never felt it was my destiny to serve 30 years. However, as the years passed by, this view changed, and I believed I was destined to do it. Yes, we came across people who respected nothing, not even themselves, but in the main, they knew when it was a fair cop and eventually complied, however, towards the end of my career I went through a very difficult time, but that's for another chapter.

Humour went alongside the darker side of the job as a necessary relief. You do laugh at some things that go on in the job and it helps to keep you sane. On one occasion, just after finishing my probation, I was out in a car with my partner. We had set our stall out to catch a prolific disqualified driver who had been banned for two years by the Courts. He had shown no respect for this ban and drove around his village and locality with total impunity.

We laid in wait at a junction where I knew there was a good chance, we would see him driving. I also knew that if he saw us, he would speed off. The adrenaline was pumping around my body in anticipation of catching him. We waited for some 50 minutes and then he appeared. He was extremely street wise and although we had done our best to hide our marked police car, he immediately saw us and accelerated away at high speed. The pursuit was on. We quickly reached speeds of 70 mph and as we entered a sharp corner, I realised we were travelling too fast into it. Touching the brakes resulted in me losing complete control of the car. Speed mixed with an adverse camber and a wet road resulted in the car feeling as though we were on a skid pan.

Everything now felt as though we were in slow motion, and I knew we were going to have a horrific accident. Our car spun 360 degrees twice, hit an embankment and then rolled over several times, during which I honestly thought we were going to die. The noise and velocity of the impact were unbelievable. We ended up coming to a stop with the vehicle resting on its roof. Upside down and trapped in the vehicle, I looked sideways at my partner and was so relieved to see he was still alive. I tried in vain to use the vehicle's VHF radio to shout for assistance, but of course I had obliterated any ariels in the smash. My partner said, "the radio won't work" and once I realised about the ariels I said, "No Shit Sherlock" We both laughed. It was a relief to know we were both alive.

We eventually managed to get out of the car and could clearly see that the scene was one of carnage. I had damaged the police car beyond repair, with no panels being left intact. All of its windows were smashed, and I can remember thinking "what the hell have I done" The suspect had not experienced such misfortune and as the ambulance arrived, I knew this would have severe consequences for me.

A few days later, other officers arrested the suspect, and he went to trial, charged with driving whilst disqualified and failing to stop for the police. During that time, I had my driving permit suspended and wasn't allowed to drive any police vehicles. When the suspect's case went to Court, he pleaded not guilty and was represented by an eloquent solicitor. So eloquent, in fact, that the Magistrates found the suspect not guilty of all of his charges.

Now I'm not a lover of defence solicitors, especially the ones defending suspects I'm trying to convict. That said, however, this solicitor was as sharp as a knife and his performance had impressed me. As the dust settled on the verdict and the suspect left the Court, I approached his solicitor and asked for a quiet word. I explained to him that because of my crash and the serious nature of the accident, I was to be summonsed to Court for driving without due care and attention. It's of significance that this was a time when there was no training in vehicle pursuits. A basic driving course is all that I had completed, so understanding adverse cambers and critical speeds on corners was something else.

I slightly bemused the solicitor when I explained my predicament and the fact that I was asking if he would represent me. Weeks later, we were back at the same Court, but this time he was my solicitor, and now I was the defendant. You couldn't write it. The solicitor explained that although excess speed had been a primary causation of the accident; the speed alone wasn't an offence because of my being in lawful pursuit of the suspect.

Realising that the pursuit was becoming too dangerous and aborting it at a critical position on the bend had been the catalyst for the police car losing control. After a relatively quick trial, the Magistrates then went to preside over my case. I knew if they found me guilty, it was unlikely that I would face a jail sentence, but I didn't know if I would lose my driving licence. What was going to happen to my career?

After 20 tense minutes, the Magistrates returned and gave their verdict.... Not guilty. I can't express the relief I felt. I've often wondered since; how many police officers and suspected criminals have used the same solicitor for charges related to the same incident with the same outcome? It's too ironic to believe.

Once back at work, I remember checking my work tray to find a scrap piece of paper with the words "you can now drive police vehicles" written on it and signed by my Inspector. Great, six months of carrying the burden of a trial around with me, gone in six words. There was no asking me if I felt confident driving again.

Within a week, I was involved in another fail to stop incident. As we pursued the car, my heart was beating furiously at the stress of the situation. I wanted to stop the stolen car I was pursuing, but I was still reeling from my recent prosecution and didn't want to have another accident. I had received no additional training in-between, and like anyone with any sense, the first accident had made me more wary. My self-confidence had been knocked. It was a tough time for me. Thankfully, after 10 minutes of high-speed driving, we stopped the car and arrested the occupants.

In the 90s, a lot of traffic cops were ex-army personnel and quite regimental in their appearance and outlook on policing. So, this day, as a rookie cop, I was out with one such officer.

I got out of the car and hadn't put my helmet on. When I got back in, he asked. 'Where is your helmet? Why aren't you wearing it?' I apologise and he comments. 'You should wear it, especially in Garforth. A Divisional Commander lives around here.'

Back in the car, we are up near Gipton in Leeds, and we see a car driven by a man who my partner knows is an active criminal. It looks as though he's going to fail to stop, but as we get close to him, he heads into a cul-de-sac so couldn't escape. The cop I'm with tells me to get ready because he believes the lad will run. Just prior to the imminent stopping of the suspect's vehicle, I ask, 'Shall I put my helmet on?' 'Fuck your helmet', he barks at me, 'just get out and get hold of him.'

One of the funniest incidents I attended was when I was on foot beat. It was an early shift; the control room had asked me to go to a car accident involving a dog. The poor thing had been run over. By the time I arrived, the car involved had gone, but the dog was still limping about. It's a dark winter's morning and I'm left thinking about what I'm going to do with the dog. Just then, the dog walks off down a driveway and sits at the side door of the house.

I was so pleased. It obviously lived there. It was only 6.30am, but I realised they must have let it out of the property, or it had got loose from its kennel. I knocked on the door. After a few minutes, the occupant answered, still in her dressing gown. The dog darted past her and into the house. I apologised for waking her up and explained that her poor dog, or I should say, began to explain, when I looked at the injured dog who, still in shock, wretched up a pile of sick on a beautiful white rug in the middle of the living room.

I'm feeling so sorry for this poor, shaking animal, but I continue to tell her what's happened to her beloved pet. She listens, looking somewhat bemused, and says, 'I don't own a dog.' We are both looking at the dog and the vomit on her rug. Eventually I think she saw the funny side, as did I. I then ended up taking the dog to the vets where the actual owners came forward to claim it.

There is, of course, the serious side of the job. The no-nonsense tough policing. I can't remember the number of hangings, suicides and sudden deaths they have sent me to deal with, along with the never-ending victims of crime and hardened criminals. There are just too many to recall. The longer you are in the job, the more impact these things can have on you. During the 30 years I served, I was assaulted on hundreds of occasions. I know some officers are affected by what they encounter, but I can say yes; it was a weight for me, but one I was, for most of the time, comfortable carrying. I wasn't seeing anything more than I expected to see, so

I knew, or thought I knew, that my mindset was in the right place.

I have to say, and I think most cops would agree, that the self-generated arrests were what I thrived on. They gave me an opportunity to use my initiative and further develop the skills an excellent police officer should possess. You could say I was proud of my uniform and what it stood for. That would sadly change in the distant future.

Chapter 4-Devil in the Detail

'The Devil is always in the detail, always look beyond the obvious'

Like many people, I had heard of the idiom. 'The Devil is in the Detail' but never really thought much about its meaning. I had no need to. A dictionary will tell you it refers to a hidden element, not initially noticed. I quickly learned as a police officer, it meant that you never accept that you have got all the evidence on the first look without taking the time and to get down to the real detail.

As mentioned in chapter one, I was so lucky to have a tutor with 20 years' service and experience. He had seen and done a lot. It didn't matter to me why he had been demoted. I knew I could gain from that. He was a rough diamond and knew all the tricks used by criminals to escape justice.

My initiation into how important 'the devil is in the detail' really came the day we were sent to a call where a woman had rung in, informing us, her eighty plus year-old next-door neighbour was being harassed by a man in a van. She also added that he had two children with him.

We arrive at the scene to find a gypsy there who had obviously been lopping the old lady's trees. He had used his nine and ten-year-old children to go up the trees and lop them. The job she had agreed to was being done. The allegations started when the man asked for £200 when £20 had initially been agreed.

That could be seen by some officers as a civil matter now, but Tony, my tutor, arrested him for attempting to obtain monies by deception. We arranged for the children to be taken to a place of safety. We booked the man into custody and then returned to the scene to get a statement from the old lady. I can remember being a little perplexed when Tony took a lengthy statement from her. Back at the station, Tony spent a good hour or more interviewing the suspect before putting him back in his cell.

'Why do you think I've spent so long getting a detailed statement from the victim?' he asked me. I didn't really have a clue. I was also unsure why the suspect's interview had gone on for over an hour. The crux of the case to me was what we call word versus word. His word against hers. Had he tried to deceive her? Tony agreed with me but explained if this case goes to Court, yes, it's word versus word but, his defence solicitor or barrister dependent on if it is Magistrates or Crown Court, will try to portray the old lady as not been in charge of her faculties. He will say she is a little deaf, senile, and slightly forgetful. Now, look at some of the nineteen questions asked of the suspect when he was interviewed.

'Did you turn up in a white van?'

'Yes, I did.' He replies.
'Did the van have an orange light on?'

'Yes, it did.' He replies.

'Did you have two children?'

'Yes, I did. They're my children.'

'Did you say to the lady, do you want your trees lopping missus?'

'Yes, I would have said that.'

Tony went through all the points and questions asked and said.' The only point in dispute in both of their accounts relates to the amount of money they agreed for him completing the work. It became clear, inadvertently; the gypsy, in his own answers, corroborated by the victim, had shown her to be of sound body and mind. Not deaf, not confused, but a first-class witness.

Why has she not remembered the price when she had total recall of all the other eighteen questions? That discussion tuned me into a different type of investigator. It sharpened me up. I took nothing at face value from that moment on. I knew there would be a lot more lurking below the surface; it was just knowing how to detect it.

Whilst the suspect was in custody, Tony's experience came to the fore again. As he suspected, the male had given us false details. Nowadays, electronic fingerprints can be sent off immediately. Within an hour, we can confirm someone's identity. Back then, however, it was paper, and ink and results took several weeks to come back.

We successfully got him remanded into custody and into jail until his trial date. His fingerprints revealed he was wanted for several other serious deception offences. Had Tony not seen beyond the surface and pursued the case, none of that would become known. It was real top-drawer stuff.

Now I have to say that although the protection we could give to allay the fears in the victim that the gypsy may seek revenge was almost nil, we recognised she had a very good relative and neighbour who helped to look after her. We also provided some reassurance visits to her home address for the next several weeks.

The suspect was sentenced to seven years' imprisonment. It was a fantastic result. It reassured the pensioner, knowing the suspect was going to be in jail for some considerable time because of the other serious criminal offences he had been wanted for. The Crown Prosecution didn't pursue her case. We agreed with the prosecutor that the suspect's sentence for these other offences wouldn't be any longer because of our victim's case. This way, she wouldn't need to attend Court. It was a great relief to her.

Another time 'the devil in the detail' came into play was when we drove past a garden centre that regularly got burgled. We saw two lads walking along the street. Nothing unusual then, other than it was 2am in the morning and Garforth is a rural, quiet place. So, as we approach, I'm looking for things that could be suspicious. Then I see one of them drop something.

We stop them, get their details, then I look to see what one of them had dropped. It's a fully wrapped sweet. Now why would someone drop an untouched sweet still in its wrapper when they see the police? Something wasn't right, so we detained the lads whilst we checked their details. Neither was wanted, but we knew them both well and knew they were active criminals. We searched them but found nothing of note on them. A lot of officers would have ended the encounter at that stage. Although we were several hundred yards away from the Garden Centre, I recalled they sold similar kinds of sweets in the cafe. Whilst we stayed with them, another unit checked the Garden Centre.

The officers discovered the premises phone and alarm wires had been cut and disabled. At the side of the cafe were thousands of pounds worth of property hidden in barrels, ready to go. One lad had helped himself to a handful of sweets, including the one still in his pocket, whilst in the cafe. When we saw them, they were on their way to where they had parked their car, ready to go back to get the stolen property.

On seeing our marked police car, the suspect panicked and dropped the sweet to get rid of the evidence. All I'm thinking is why have you done that? Now, had he not done this, although we would have still stopped them because of the time of night, we would have never uncovered the nearby burglary. I would have had nothing to detain and subsequently arrest them for.

These were real professionals; they had worked it all out. Parked their car a mile away so as not to arouse suspicion whilst they were inside the Garden Centre. Easy then to go back and collect what they had stolen, which was already in barrels, ready to load into their car. The three and a half years prison sentence they received tells you they had previous convictions for similar offences.

Another example is when I was on the Regional Roads Crime Team. We had stopped a car. Nothing consequential, really. My partner was checking it out for insurance. I'm in the driver's seat of the police car and look across the road to see a woman sat in a stationary car. It's a nice day in June and warm. She sits there, alone, nothing out of the ordinary, nothing suspicious.

Then we looked at each other. She immediately put her tinted window fully up. I thought, why do that on a warm day when you've seen me? What have you got to be worried about? Okay, some people worry when they see a police car behind them. They suddenly drive three miles under the speed limit, but this was a stationary car.

I get out of my vehicle and walk across to the woman. I ask if it is her vehicle and point out the dark tinted driver's window may be illegal. I'm thinking, however, there's more than this beneath the surface. We checked her and the vehicle on the Police National computer. We find nothing out of the ordinary. But it revealed there was some interest in her. At some point, she had been of interest to the financial investigation team as they had placed a marker on her. The rapid increase in money laundering means these types of markers are now quite common.

I was aware I had no powers to search her or the vehicle and was up front with her. I told her I had checked her details and found that they linked her to previous police financial enquiries. I then ask her if she has any large amounts of cash in the car. 'I've a bit of money in the glove box.' Comes the reply. With consent, she shows me what's in the glove box. 'I don't know how much is there, it's my dad's' she says. There looks to be over a thousand pounds.

Suspicions aroused, but I'm still not sure. I ask if I can speak to her dad to clarify if he is aware and happy about such a lot of his money being in the glove compartment. She agrees, rings her dad's number on her mobile, and hands it to me. I tell him there is nothing to worry about. He is happy speaking with me. Then I ask him if he can tell me if there was anything that belongs to him in the car. 'Anything of value?' Instantly, he then claims he can't understand me, and then puts down the phone.

It would have been easy to leave things there, but I'm not happy and think back to what my tutor Tony would have done. I have a female who is clearly very nervous and in possession of a substantial amount of cash she claims belongs to her father. She has no explanation for carrying such an amount of cash. Her father corroborates nothing and then refuses to speak to me. It gives me enough suspicion to arrest her on suspicion of possession of criminal property (the money). I go with it.

So, she's arrested, booked into custody and I get an Inspector's authority to search her house. Another £78,000, hidden in a purpose made cupboard behind some clothing in her bedroom, is discovered. Now we have something very tangible. I give myself credit for my instinct, but this was nothing compared to the credit of the financial investigator detective who got the job to investigate.

It took 18 months for the investigation to be completed, but it concluded that daughter and father had been involved in mortgage application frauds. It turned out that they had accumulated £275,000 by criminal means. The cash seized from the vehicle was part of that fraud. It's a prime example of looking beyond the surface. Putting that window up cast a shadow across my mind, and I needed to remove that shadow. That one attention to detail brought a stop to a well-established mortgage fraud and landed two criminals in jail.

A further example of attention to detail is when I was out with a Special Constable. Specials are volunteers with the same arrest powers as regular officers. It was a chilly night, around Christmas time, and I pulled up beside a car with tinted windows and noticed the passenger window was down by a good two inches. I'm thinking, why would you have a window open on a night as cold as this unless you wanted to let something in the car out?

We adopt the usual practice to follow the car and run it through the systems to make sure there are no markers we need to be aware of. The car stops. We are in Leeds City Centre. A big man gets out. I see he is the only person in the vehicle. He locks the car and walks over to me. 'Why have you stopped me?' he asks. I tell him it's because a check on the car shows nine people linked to its insurance, and I need to make sure he is one of them. That amount of named persons on one insurance policy is quite rare. He retorts immediately. 'Well, I am insured.'

Now it's becoming quite clear that he wants to put distance between me and his car. What makes me think this? Normally, a stopped driver waits for us to tell them to step out of the car and then will sit with us in our vehicle whilst we conduct the roadside checks. This guy is instantly straight out of the car, which he immediately locks up. He then walks over to me. I notice he has an SIA badge on. If you don't know what that is, it's the badge to show you are a licensed security door personnel.

'You're not searching my car.' He then pipes up. Well, I haven't said that I am going to search his car, so why is he so keen to tell me I'm not? He continues to tell me I have no authority to search it. It has me really thinking now. Windows down, you don't want me to search your car and at that stage I had no powers to do so. However, on further speaking to him, a strong smell of cannabis was evident on his clothing.

'My son smokes weed, it's not me.' He tells me when faced with facts. Reasonable suspicion had now tipped over. I tell him he's being detained for a drugs search, I put handcuffs on him. He's a big guy, so I take no chances. I am entitled to handcuff someone if I think they may run or cause me any problems. So, I have not arrested him, I'm detaining him so my partner can search his car.

Low and behold, well-hidden underneath the back seat is a large amount of cannabis, later established to be worth over £4000. I now arrest him, and another criminal is off the streets all because of a window being two inches down on a cold winter's night. As an officer, you must be more than just aware of your immediate surroundings, you must be switched on and at the top of your game to be really effective. Once again, I'm out in a vehicle with a Special Constable. After a ten hour, mostly uneventful shift, I'm about to take the exit for junction 41 to head for our police base at Carr Gate. We are in an unmarked car on the M1 with a 50-mph speed restriction because of road works being carried out. This silver Audi comes past us at around 70 mph. We decide to have a look at it. It's a car from the Northeast. We get closer and stop it. The vehicle contains two males.

After obtaining the males' details, it was clear both had intelligence linked to them for previous firearms offences. Both men are compliant, and we place the driver in our vehicle. I ask him what the rush is regarding his speed, and he states he is on the way back to Newcastle after visiting his brother in Nottingham. He says that his father has recently passed away, and he needed to sort out some family business regarding his will. Now I have travelled from the Northeast on hundreds of occasions and with the timeline of the journey he's giving me, it left him with only 30 minutes to speak to his brother.

I leave him with my colleague and go to his car to check it out and speak with the passenger. His story is different, similar, but the timeline is out of sync. I notice that his heart is beating fast through the thin t-shirt he is wearing. The detail again! He's clearly very nervous. I see nothing in the car at first glance, so go back to sit with the driver.

I tell him from my experience as a police officer I suspect that he's lying to me. He tells me he's not. Now and then, I smell a strange odour coming from him. It's like a perfume smell, I'm trying to work it out. I can't tell what it is but suspect it may be controlled drugs. I know I have two people with two different stories, and that gives me sufficient suspicion to search them and the vehicle. They are out of their force area; they have got previous convictions. Their recent accounts for the journey differ considerably. The passenger is clearly extremely nervous. I know I'm pushing my powers of search, but I have justification.

We handcuff both the driver and passenger and detain them. As I search the car, professionally hidden, where the spare tyre should be, I find two self-sealed tubes about a foot long. Inside, I see white powder. It turns out to be £40000 of M-CAT. That was the odour I could smell on the driver. M-CAT or Mephedrone is a high-powered stimulant along the same lines as Cocaine and Ecstasy. A Class B drug and illegal. Possession can bring with it up to 5 years in jail but dealing it can get up to 14 years inside.

Where they had really been was London to pick up the drugs and they were on their way back home, but tiredness and the need to get home had caused the driver to speed and that one mistake brought him to our attention and to their downfall.

Today, I don't think front-line officers have the time to look thoroughly at such a situation. The workload and number of calls to the police are so great. Most officers' abilities to conduct self-generated stops like this one are very limited because they have to respond to a high volume of calls. The pressure is immense. It's like a tsunami. Policing styles have had to change. Satisfaction levels are not the same with officers and the public. What the public view as good policing has all but gone.

I remember a time when you would get people coming up to you and giving you information and intelligence. They wouldn't want their names mentioning, but they did their public duty. You would be told if someone was drink driving or drug dealing. Now, there is a big gulf between society and the police, not because officers don't want to serve the public. They do as I've said before, it's workloads and call handling that holds them back.

I have often begun duty and less than two hours into my shift, I've heard the radio operative say, 'Inspector, there are now seven 999 calls outstanding with no available units to attend them.' The next shift come on and not only have they to deal with these calls but also their own calls. It has changed the way the public view us in terms of our ability to respond. They feel we are letting them down, and we are.

Two years before I retired, they diagnosed me with type two diabetes, and I had to let my supervision know about this condition. It meant that I had to keep a careful check on my blood sugar levels and diet. I remember starting duty at 6am one day. I'd done a self-generated drug warrant and was dealing with the prisoner and investigation. I hadn't had a meal or drink and it was now getting on for 2.30pm. I knew I needed to get something to eat. I hadn't eaten since 4.30am when I had got up and I wasn't due to finish work until 4pm.

After completing the investigation, I sat down to commence my meal break. I could hear on the radio the control room repeatedly requesting the need for officers to attend a 999-emergency call. Again, there were no response officers to attend, all were committed to other calls.

The control room shouted my collar number out and informed me I had to attend the call. I explained I had been on duty for nearly nine hours and was about to get a meal. Silence, then the words from supervision, 'you have to attend this call.' I spoke to supervision and reminded them I hadn't eaten for nearly nine hours and had recently been diagnosed with diabetes. Nothing changed. They still instructed me to go to the call. I set off to the job in a van but on route had a collision. It was clearly my fault and was down to my lack of concentration and perhaps my sugar levels dropping from not eating.

The devil in the detail took time and effort, and that was being eroded. Few now had the time to make that effort. I knew it, and I wasn't the only one. We were heading towards breaking point, but few had the guts to stand up and tell anyone in the hierarchy. Would it have made any difference? I don't know. I know we weren't giving the public anywhere near the service they needed or deserved.

Sixteen years' earlier, I had stood up to be counted. It was at the Police Federation Conference, attended by hundreds of officers and many senior ones from other forces, including our own Chief Constable. I put forward my personal observations and views. By that time, I had been in the force for twelve years. Ten of which had been on the beat. I had seen how things were changing, and not for the better. I remained positive, as most police officers do, but I had realised that it was no longer the career I had envisaged or would want my son, then nine years old, to follow.

I explained job satisfaction was at an all-time low for many officers, and this was in the main down to chronic staffing shortages. I gave examples where due to demand and the lack of supply, there had often been no officers left on the beat. I outlined the feelings of hopelessness as officers face pages and pages of delayed calls. I told of my concern for investigations I saw as suffering, unfinished because of the next urgent job. I made a point about the Crown Prosecution Service and the inadequate sentences being given out. My points were all accepted. Nothing came of them. The only response I remember was an Inspector sarcastically saying it surprised him I hadn't been sacked after raising my concerns.

Another officer reiterated the same angst I had expressed. He was working as a response officer, which he called his sentence. Why? Because to him, that was how it felt 95% of the time. The officer made a passionate plea to be heard. Outlining the good days as being very rare compared to the bad ones, the ones he remembered. It showed a lot of despair in his words. He couldn't provide, when asked, an example of good policing, nor could he recall a day when he could say, 'It's not so bad.' It was that bad.

So, I must ask. How can you concentrate on the devil in the detail when the detail requires quality investigative time and attention to unpick? And that time is rarely now afforded to today's front-line officers.

Chapter 5-Both Sides of the Fence

'Crime doesn't give a damn who it hurts, how or why'

1996 saw me join the drugs team, based at Killingbeck Police station. By that time, I had served six years in the police. I felt confident. I had seen most things, and I knew a lot about criminals and their way of life. I was now ready to experience something different. I saw it as a new opportunity to use a fresh set of investigation skills. As a bonus, John Gee, a detective on the Team, was a good friend and colleague of mine. I instinctively knew joining the team was a good move, and I wanted to be part of it. Looking back to that time now makes me realise how naïve I was to the drugs world; however, it didn't take me long to recognise the power of addiction and what addicts will do for their next fix.

Drugs, heroin in particular, have a damning and evil effect on users. I had no comprehension of the devastating influence drugs had on people's lives. Not just users, but their families and victims of the crimes they commit offences against in order to feed their habit. I knew drug use was on the increase and a vast amount of crime was linked to it, but I had no idea how bad it was until I joined the team. It was a big eye opener for me.

Learning was on the job; we had a great Sergeant who would take me to one side and explain how things were done. I would work with a partner who had experience, and it didn't take long for me to pick things up. One thing that was new to me was working with informants. I had no experience of this but soon recognised the importance and advantages of these sources in tackling drug crime.

Informants were usually addicts or members of the public living in and amongst the ravages of drug infested communities. Some were parents of addicts wanting to make some sort of difference in the impact drugs had made to their children's lives. If the information they provided got results, they would receive a small amount of money. They were happy, and we got the information we needed. The system worked well for us.

After a few weeks, I realised that heroin was the deadliest drug we were coming into contact with. The common misperception that drug users come from bad backgrounds is untrue. Users come from every section of society. Drugs don't differentiate between the haves and have nots. Once heroin takes over, they have a bond, and that's the squalid existence they live. It holds them fast in a perpetual cycle of stealing in order to sell or trade the stolen property for drugs. That's all that matters.

It's a different type of criminality taking place. Normally, criminals are committing an offence for personal gain. They want wealth to lead a lifestyle they feel society owes them. Drug crime, where users are concerned, is for one purpose, the next fix, high, whatever you want to call it. For many, the only personal gain is a premature death or an existence of long-term misery. It would be hard for someone not to have some feeling of empathy with them. That doesn't mean I condone their choices or feel they have a right to steal from innocent people to feed their habits. I don't and never could.

I felt I had a real purpose, and I knew I would put all of my energy into stopping the blatant dealing taking place on the streets of Leeds. I knew I wouldn't stop the addicts being addicts. In fact, in all of my years of policing, with one exception, I never knew of a person who got off and stayed off heroin. The only exception to this was a man called Paul Hannaford, who I would end up championing many years later. He was a high-end user with a habit of £500 a day but living down South. In amongst the hundreds of addicts I met in Leeds, I never witnessed any of them getting off and staying off heroin.

The work was hard but rewarding. When I started, I would set out to identify as many as possible of those who dealt drugs on a street level. One of the simple ways to achieve this was through covert (hidden and unknown by others), and overt (in plain view) surveillance. Many of the initial investigations began at phone boxes around 10am. That's the time you knew the addicts would be desperate for their first fix of the day and here was where they would arrange a rendezvous with their dealers. The pattern was always the same. The addict would make a quick phone call to the dealer's mobile phone and minutes later, a vehicle would pull up. They would exchange cash for the drug and within seconds, the deal was done.

As I witnessed such deals whilst being undercover, I noticed most addicts would look white and pale faced and in a dreadfully emaciated state. Many looked like death warmed up, extremely thin and with very poor complexions. I often felt for them and their families that they had ended up looking like they did. Yes, it was their choice that had got them to this, but their families were also casualties in this wrong choice.

Due to this choice and their addiction, a long-term addict had usually lost all close friends and family along with any materialistic possessions. Every day they carried the burden of how to relieve the desperation for their next fix. The only company they now had was the company of other addicts. Many would shop lift to fund their daily addiction, often referring to this as their grafting (working).

Driving the drugs vehicles would be a runner, a small fish in a large pond. These are individuals who would get paid a wage mainly in the form of drugs. Many of these would be addicts themselves. The real profit makers, creaming in thousands of pounds a day, wouldn't risk being caught and their workers, if arrested, wouldn't dare give them up. To do so would put their own lives in danger.

To compare the different lifestyles of the addicts to those running a drug business was worlds apart. One drug dealer, I recall, was registered as unemployed but was driving a flashy sports car every time we stopped him. When searched, he never had less than £600 on him in used banknotes. He had a team of around six lads who worked tirelessly from morning to night delivering drugs to his customers.

There were many disappointments in the early days of the operation. The simple task of stopping those suspected of dealing drugs didn't net the quick rewards I had hoped for. If we tried to stop the dealers after an exchange, they would drive off at high speed and think nothing of swallowing the small wraps of heroin they carried in their mouths.

They never carried large amounts of drugs at any one time. A wrap, (one deal), would contain 0.4 gms of heroin and would be tightly wrapped in cellophane. It was possible for a street dealer to hold up to 20 such wraps in his mouth or anal passage. During this time, I was spending a lot of emotional energy and watched any innocence I had left being swallowed up by the evil environment I was working in.

The last vestige of which disappeared during a drugs raid at a house. Often, drugs would be hidden in fridge freezers. Searching the fridge, I was curious to know what was in the three small vials of clear liquid I had found here. The female occupant of the house informed me it was methadone, a heroin substitute. When I pressed her for further information, she stated that because she had become pregnant whilst injecting heroin, her baby had also been born with a heroin addiction.

It sickens me to think about it, even now. Over 20 years later. The baby had been born an addict because of the mother taking drugs during her pregnancy. An innocent little child. I'll never, to my dying day, forget that moment. A new-born destroyed by a drug, it had no knowledge or understanding of the pure evil of heroin cannot be any clearer than in this case.

As the operation continued, we obtained more evidence against those involved in the sale of drugs and could then start to build a case against them. There is no honour amongst thieves is a common but very true saying. The ones delivering the drugs were too frightened to speak to us, but the users themselves were a different story. All they wanted to know was that we would give them anonymity.

After many long hours of covert observations, we obtained a good break. A flat in Saxton Gardens, Leeds, was identified as a main contact point for heroin sales. We had set ourselves up in a nearby unoccupied flat and would arrive early to avoid being detected. The last thing we needed was for the dealers to be tipped off by local residents. It was clear that the flat we were in had once belonged to an elderly person. It made me think how much change that person had witnessed take place in their lifetime for drugs to have now ravaged his neighbourhood to the extent they had done.

At the 10am magic hour, the users arrived in their droves. Desperate for their fixes. So many were turning up that the photographer who was with us, at times couldn't keep up with the pace needed to get the photographic evidence of what was unfolding beneath us. The only person who didn't appear was one of the main subjects of the operation. It looked like success was going to evade us again, but then I picked up a crucifix I had noticed laid flat on a chair, and I prayed hard that God would help our cause.

Ten minutes later the suspect we had been waiting for arrived. A taxi dropped him off and he went into the watched location. A surprise search was then put into operation at the flat, resulting in the seizure of a substantial amount of heroin. Arrested and convicted, he gained an eighteen-month prison sentence into the bargain. After that, we arrested others who had been linked to the investigation. It's a good feeling knowing you are ridding the streets of people who don't care about the consequences of their actions.

In the early days, when success was rare, and we had more failures than triumphs, any arrest and conviction made the hard work worthwhile. We were still putting the pieces of the jigsaw together then, a necessary task by a very dedicated team. Arrests would come as we slotted together the pieces in the operation.

I never took my eye off the ball whilst on the team. To make sure that I remained focused, I used to take the photographs we had of the drug dealers and pin them upon the office wall. It reminded me daily of the amount of effort still required to get these people off the streets.

We were determined to defeat them, one by one, until we had taken every mug shot down.

We knew that trying to catch the dealers would stretch us to the limit and was unlikely to be successful, so we targeted the users. We knew from experience that most would give us a statement using a pseudonym. One well educated lad who did this looked nothing like a heroin user. I asked him what his story was. He told me he could get off the drug and stay clean for as long as 18 months, but it was always there in his mind. Something would then happen, and he would use again.

Your heart sinks hearing such stories because you know that heroin is like the Devil. It grips and grips you until it takes your soul, destroying all in its path. The users, their families, the victims, no one is spared. It has no moral compass, just a need to dominate and wipe out everyone and everything it could.

We had some good arrests, and there was a great camaraderie in the team. I enjoyed what I was doing.

I felt I was helping, albeit in a small way, to clean the streets of those dealing so much misery to others. There were even times when the outcome of an operation was quite humorous. I can think back to V97, the music concert at Temple Newsam. Our team was asked to mingle amongst the party goers. Now there were hundreds of thousands of people there across three days, all spread out in fields with various stages for some of the top bands in the country. Friday, Saturday, Sunday. Our remit, mingle into the crowds and find the drug dealers.

So, there I am, bandana on, shorts and t-shirt. It's a lovely summer evening and I look nothing like the part, but it was the best I could manage. On our team is also a woman called Caroline, who is milling around the same as the rest of us. She comes up and says there is a black lad in one dance tent openly selling E's. For anyone who doesn't know what Es are, it's a drug called MDMA, commonly known as ecstasy or molly. Mostly taken recreationally to get a high, giving the user hallucinations and sometimes a heightened sense of relaxation.

Anyway, we set off on mass to find this lad, but because of the sheer numbers of party goers, we got separated from one another and it ended up with just Caroline and me searching for him. I then see her talking to a black male and I realise this is the suspect. I keep my distance, but he's as crafty as a rattlesnake. He has no intention of doing a deal outside the tent, so guides her inside. I follow them where there are hundreds of dancers and music is blasting out.

John's recollection is slightly different from mine. John will tell you he found my bandana quite something. He is outside the tent; I add. He can't come in because he looks like some ageing hippy. We both remember vividly the guy walking around the dance tent with a little bag, shouting. 'Come on, get your E's, ten pound a tab.' Like he was selling sunglasses. Caroline's with him trying to do a deal, John's watching from the side-lines and I'm staying within striking distance.

John tells me he then sees the guy looking at me as if to say, 'something weird about him'. John thinks it was my appearance that made him suspicious. 'A big stocky man, wearing a bandana who couldn't dance. Jigging around like a loony' is how he described me. The man looked over at me, but then looked away. I'm thinking you really have no idea what's going to happen next, do you? With hindsight, neither did I. He clearly didn't suspect anything as the next thing he did was hand Caroline something and she then grabs hold of him.

Now he's only about 5'4" but built like a brick shit house. He makes off, dragging Caroline with him. She keeps hold, and he bites her arm. By which time I've got involved. We are on the floor grappling; I've got him and drag him over. For several minutes, I keep him on the floor, but he's determined to get away. We're both strong and well-built. He's just shorter than me. I have to use all of my strength to keep him on the ground, as I know once he's up and able to use his body to punch and attack, I'm in trouble.

Those seven minutes of struggling felt like seventy at the time. Thankfully the concert's security staff arrive, and we get him handcuffed and arrest him. Found in his possession were a packet of white tablets with the

Mitsubishi car emblem stamped on them. This was the popular motif that was stamped on the E tablets at that time. There's only about 20 in the packet he has, but he also has a thousand pounds in cash.

He's arrogant and full of himself, but eventually John and I interview him. He tells us it's a Mickey Mouse job and we'll prove nothing. I tell him we don't have to, there's an officer he's offered to supply drugs, to, and that's all we need to prove.

After the interview, he mellows a bit and tells us what we will find when we send the drugs off for forensic testing. With a grin, he tells us the tablets aren't drugs but paracetamol. He's got a mate who stamped the Mitsubishi emblem on them, and he then sold them at ten pounds a go.

So here is this guy selling common everyday paracetamol tables disguised as Ecstasy, to ravers across the country for a tenner a pop and then disappearing before party goers realised, they'd been done. Ecstasy tablets take around an hour to affect the user, and that's when he was just about to leave the concert.

Well, he thinks he's got away with it, but there's an old-fashioned offence. 'Going equipped to cheat' along with attempting to supply a controlled drug to another. It matters not that the item was paracetamol, the fact that he had claimed he was supplying a drug to Caroline made him guilty of the offence. He's charged, and the following morning the Stipendiary Magistrate at Leeds sends him to Armley Jail. There he languished for six months, forgotten about.

John is now retired and a good friend. He and I have often laughed, reminiscing about the days on the drugs team. There was one time when we were in an unmarked car, and we stopped these two lads in another car. One claimed to be a property developer. He wasn't. It was a load of shite. They had a bit of money on them, but not loads of cash. A few hundred quid, but I just knew I was going to see the "property developer" again.

A few weeks later, a colleague comes to our office and tells me that someone is at the front counter wanting to give some information. I go to see him and take him into a private room, and I can see he's a decent man. He tells me he's concerned about some of his neighbours. It turns out this is a couple who both have learning difficulties.

The man has seen a car pull up and go to the door of his neighbours. He thinks this is suspicious, so later goes to see what it's about. The couple tell him the man who visited earlier has asked them to look after a mobile phone for him and they are ordered not to tell anyone where it is because it's such an expensive phone.

He gives me as many details as he can. The car registration number, description of the man and the address of the vulnerable couple. The first thing I do is run the number plate through the police systems. Bingo. Something about it told me I'd seen it before. Up it pops. It's the same car that the property developer had previously been in. I don't mess about. I'm straight down to Leeds Magistrate's for a warrant to be sworn out to go search the couple's house.

At the house, we don't arrest the couple because we had credible evidence that they were totally innocent of any crime. They immediately hand us the mobile phone box, but instead of a phone; it contains several thousand pounds' worth of cocaine. Thanks to a watchful neighbour, we inherited a great job. The suspect got convicted for possession of controlled drugs with intent to supply. I had his car number plate, so he didn't deny he had dropped it off, but said he didn't know where it came from. The box itself had his and three other organised criminal fingerprints on it and subsequent arrests of these other suspects were made.

I'm including this story to show you the lengths some drug dealers will go to. A totally innocent couple living contently, when some lowlife comes up to the door, knocks and embroils them in criminal activity. They would have had no idea what was going on when the police arrived and searched their home. Do the dealers care? Of course not.

Did they have the decency to exonerate the couple of any crime? Of course not. Money is their only God.

Whilst it's not fun for anyone to be exploited in such a way, there was a comical side to it. There was a ban on overtime at work when this was going on, but by the time I'd got the warrant, seized the drugs, got back to the station and frantically completed all the administration work, without running into overtime, I'd forgotten about the unmarked Police car I had travelled in. I'd left the house in another car driven by another officer and with so many tasks to cram in before my shift finished, I'd somehow forgotten about my own car.

Next morning, I go into the office still feeling good. It's early and I'm ready to start again when a detective from the CID office asks me if I have the car keys for the unmarked car, I'd booked out the day before. I think and try to remember, then I feel my pockets and find the car key and then think….'Oh, no, oh fucking no' runs through my brain. The detective then tells me that the vehicle had been smashed to bits and has had to be recovered by a low loader.' What can I say? The criminals down where I had parked it realised it was an unmarked police vehicle.

That's the one time I ended up getting disciplined. I was reprimanded and put in the Divisional Register for neglect of duty. It would have been cheaper to pay me the overtime!

Going back to the vulnerable couple. It was important to protect them, so when the suspect asked how we knew about the drugs, we told him there had been a warrant issued to search the house and drugs with his fingerprints on them had been recovered. He accepted that, and we didn't have to use the couple as witnesses, either. His fingerprints were on the box, the drugs and the cellophane wrapping, so it was pointless him denying it.

I'm often asked what an average day is on the drugs team. It starts early, very early, if we are going on a drug raid or other operation. Typically, we would obtain warrants based on information received or watch telephone boxes with people coming back and forth ordering drugs. However, you never knew what you were going to get from one day to another. We did get resistance, violence and threats made towards us. Did we get scared, at times? Yes, without a doubt I did.

Some dealers were more ruthless and violent than others, and you knew they would hurt you if they could.

There was this one time we had been given some information about a house where there was a wanted man and drugs being used within it. After obtaining a search warrant, we smashed the door down to find one user injecting heroin into his foot. He already had the syringe in it and finished his fix before we could stop him.

Why would he be injecting into his foot? Because common with long-term heroin users, his veins had collapsed in other areas of his body. We know this as fire in the vein. It happens when venous sclerosis sets in, and the vein becomes so hard it stops functioning. Users then have to look for other veins and will inject into their legs, hands and groin, desperate to get their next fix. With this lad, his feet were the last area he had left. It's sickening and so very sad. You know they aren't leading any kind of life, but they are breaking the law and have to be dealt with. These people are painfully existing day after day, sadly it is nothing more than that.

Let me describe a drug den for you to give you a better understanding of the life some users lead. To say it's a sad world they exist in is an understatement. The first thing you will notice is from the outside. The windows will have what look like rags or newspaper covering them. Opening the door, the stench hits you. A mixture of urine, faeces, sweat and stale blood. The atmosphere is foreboding. Syringes and soiled clothes are strewn around the floor. Addicts in various stages of undress and various states of reality slump about the place. Most have bad complexions, needle marks and bruising. They can be sat in their own defecation. When you look at the toilet, you see why. It's hard to describe how a toilet bowl can be so filthy, faeces, blood marks and urine all around the base. You wonder how these people don't gag when they walk in, but they are usually so high, they don't notice.

There is nothing glamorous in the life of an addict and, worst still, in the life of the children involved. It's not unusual to see children sat around playing with an odd toy if they are lucky. The children would usually be in a state of undress, filthy and emaciated themselves. This is when we would contact social services for some intervention. Seeing such sights when I had a young child of my own made me extremely sad and it would have been easy to walk away from it. I knew, however, that the team and I had to remain focused on our task, irrespective of what we were seeing day after day.

John and I became very accomplished at presenting a case against the drug dealers at Court. These were the people we really wanted to get, not the users. It would be an endless job. There are so many of them.

It takes a great deal of work and time to get a dealer to Court. Many hours of enquiries and surveillance lasting weeks if not months. Unless you get a lucky break, you have to be patient. A self-generated operation I worked on was at East End Park, Leeds. I knew, given enough time, it would come to fruition, and it did. It took about 18 months to get to that stage, though. You must knit it all together, link to people. Understand the connections. Have the evidence in the form of recovered drugs and photographs of drug dealing. We had thousands of photographs and observations logs.

Painstakingly you go through the photographs, linking users to dealers. Reading and re-reading notes, checking evidence. Hours and hours of police time. I recall one suspected dealer who we really wanted to get off the streets. We put the case to the Magistrate about the degradation heroin and his actions were causing and outlined why he needed to be remanded. The Magistrate agreed and placed him into custody, awaiting his trial.

I have every respect for the Leeds Magistrates. They listened intently as John and I put our cases across, so thorough was our investigation and evidencing, we always got a positive result. It gave us some hope that we were chipping away, but of course, it was only at the surface level.

The issues came once cases got to Court. We had one man charged with seven counts of supplying drugs. We had everything, including witnesses, but the Judge refused to allow them to give their accounts via a screen to protect their anonymity. That was that. There was no way they would come to Court and be identified.

We had done a tremendous amount of work, but without the witnesses, it equated to nothing. The barrister knew it; we knew it. So, he suggested, trying one last roll of the dice. He went to the defendant's barrister; he didn't mention the witnesses wouldn't be coming but offered a deal. If they would accept one drug deal instead of seven, it wouldn't go to trial. They came back and, much to our relief, accepted one deal on one day. Now in the 90s that was enough to get him a three and a half year jail sentence, but that length of sentence would be highly unlikely today.

We were always busy gathering intelligence from informants. Following up leads, doing observations. Each job would lead to others, small-time dealers would give us intelligence that would lead to getting bigger dealers to save their own skins. We knew we were onto a good thing when we arrested them and their mobile phones were ringing non-stop, indicating the scale of their drug dealing business.

So, one time, John and I were in a dealer's car that we had recovered drugs from. His mobile phone rang, and we answered it. The caller said, 'It's Tom, can you bring us one brown and white?' (Heroin and cocaine). We then went out driving the dealer's car to get evidence of the phone being used for drug deals. I'm driving it. John is in the passenger seat, and I look at him laughing. There's no way a user is going to be taken in by this grey-haired old looking man. I tell him he needs to get a beanie hat on.

Imagine this. We are sitting on Halton Moor picking up a drug user who is handing us money to purchase drugs. So, the charge would be 'attempting to purchase heroin.' We tried it in another similar case and the Court accepted it because there was no coercion on our part. We had told no one we were going to sell them drugs. They had rung a number specifically to buy drugs from someone they thought was a drug dealer. They had handed over £20 to two cops, one wearing a beanie hat, and ended up with a conviction. It wouldn't happen now, but then it was very explosive and exciting times. We were doing a good job, putting in the hours and getting some excellent results.

John will tell you that at the start we were a team of one Sergeant and one detective assisted by seven constables, and we hit the ground running. We knew there was a massive problem in East End Park, Leeds, where they handed drugs out like candy in open view of everyone, including children.

He will always say that I was passionate about the job from the word go, but he'll laugh and say I needed reining in a bit. I was so determined to try and get drugs off the streets. I always remember the advice John gave to us all. He would say, 'Ladies and Gentlemen, this is the law in relation to things we will be doing. Make sure you are up to date on it. Know it inside and out and whatever you do, you do not do it without it being a team effort. We don't need mavericks here.' I'll always think fondly of those days.

We were the foot soldiers; the Sergeant and John were at the helm. There to support us if we got upset with what we witnessed, but also there to make sure we did everything by the book. If we were doing a drug raid, for example. John would brief us with the area of law we were going to use, safety rules, and assign each one of us a role. We were so well coordinated; it was straight in. No argument, handcuff them. That was important because dealers and users would often put anything they have on them straight into their mouths and swallow it or flush it down a toilet.

How dangerous a job was it? We never underestimated it. There were drug dealers who still had some threads of respect for the law, such as not assaulting officers, but the majority were bad. They would put anything in your way to stop you from getting into a property. It was common to put a big stake of wood behind the door, knowing we would have to get through that before we could gain entry to the house. That would give them time to get rid of the drugs.

Part of John's briefing would be to watch the drains, position yourself ready to smash the fall pipe and catch the drugs if they flush them away. He used to warn us we wouldn't always be able to get in. Some of these properties had large iron bars or gates on the inside of the doors, so we couldn't get through. We then had to wait.

John reminded me once of the time we went to gain entry to a gated house but there was no way we could get in, so we used this oxy-acetylene torch to burn through the gate. It worked, but it turned out to be a plastic door and we set the house on fire. We ended up with the fire brigade there, as well as every man and his dog. We failed on that job; it would be fair to say.

Occasionally, we'd put the wrong door in because people would often take their numbers off their doors so we wouldn't know who lived where. John will tell you about a time when we smashed a door in to find a 70-year-old woman behind it screaming her head off. She had nothing to do with drugs. We had to pay for that door and the re-decoration of her hallway. How many years it knocked off her life is another thing.

The things we did to get into places were unbelievable. John once donned a postman's uniform, pressed the buzzer, and they let him in. Brilliant, thank you. Funny it may be, but you have to keep a sense of humour in a job like this. If you took everything seriously, you would end up going mad.

There was one time when we got some intelligence that there was a shipment of heroin being delivered to a house that day. We had been briefed that there were thousands of pounds in the place; they had been dealing all weekend. And the delivery was four kilos. Now that's a lot of heroin.

This house was a 'cut' house where all the deals were done. Now, these were savvy people. They had bars everywhere, even on the drainpipes, so they knew that if we raided them, they had time to get rid of the drugs, although four kilos wouldn't be easy to make disappear. We knew the suspect's car was coming from Manchester and that a certain person in the car was of interest to us. Intelligence confirmed a sighting of the car on the motorway, and we wait, parked on somebody's drive in an old vehicle so as not to draw attention to ourselves. Low and behold, the suspects arrive and take something out of the car into the house. The gates are open, and we dive in. But so did Manchester police, who had been given the same intelligence.

Undercover officers from Manchester have followed this car down the motorway and are now moving in on them. Trouble was, neither of us knew the other force was involved, so we all end up fighting each other in lumps and it ended up with us locking up one cop from Manchester. It's bedlam. He's saying, 'I'm a cop' and we're saying, 'rubbish mate, get in the car.' One of the real dealers runs off and I chase him through the estate and catch him.

After the scene from the Keystone Cops had been played out, we secured the drugs and, in time, secured prison sentences for the suspects. That may have been funny looking back, but there were also times where it turned nasty. John attempted to arrest a wanted male who had answered the door at a house but then when he realised, he was going to be arrested, punched John, who was then knocked over a hedge. The other occupants join in, the rest of our team joins in, and we are all fighting. I see this lad still assaulting John and I dive on him. I can see that John is hurt and I will not let this criminal do any more damage to him. That was one of the most frightening raids we made.

Another was a gypsy we went to arrest. A bare-knuckle fighter who still fought. In the interview, all he did was stare at John to the point we cut the interview short. John told me he really felt fear in the presence of this guy. He felt, given the chance, the man would kill him. Many years later, the man was arrested for murder.

One particular job that John and I remise about is where we went to a place called Stanks in Leeds. It's a council estate, and it was apparent that the council has grouped a lot of drug addicts together in one place. There was a girl there, 22 years old, a drug addict, a shoplifter and a prostitute. When we went in her house, there was an 18-month-old baby. It was seven in the morning and here's this youngster sat in a dirty nappy with no other clothes on. There's smashed glass all over the place. A sink full of pots. The place was absolutely filthy. No food in the fridge. Drugs are found on the premises. We whisk the child away; social services take her, and this is where the system fails. The Court gives her bail because she has a child and social services hand the little one back to her. We call at the house the following day. It's exactly the same. Social services hadn't even been to the house. I know it's not easy for them, but on this occasion, we felt they had let the child down. Why? Because the system has them run off their feet as much as we were.

Why is heroin so addictive? I have been asked. A user once described it to me and said. 'Once you are on heroin, from that first fix, you get a feeling like nothing else in the world matters and you are hooked. After that, it's all downhill. You take it then to stop the pain the addiction brings with it. Finally, you take it because your body actually needs it. You don't take it to get a high anymore but purely for the pain you are in and take something else to give you the high alongside.

It's painful to see a heroin addict coming down. They climb the walls and will sell their soul for their next fix. We will have them in the cells, and they will kick the walls, smearing them with their own faeces because they don't know what else to do, the pain is so great. They are in genuine agony; all we can do is get them medical assistance.

It's hard not to have empathy with these people, but there is a line I cannot cross. I have to be firm. We cannot condone criminal behaviour. Wrong choices have been made, but it is their choice. The power of heroin is such that I remember after years of being on the team, I started to wonder what it would be like to 'Chase the Dragon'. This is where you consume the smoke from the heroin when it is heated on silver foil. Unlike those addicted, a thought is all it remained. As I say, they have choices. We all do.

I recognised, though, that if I could think that what chance did kids have who had nothing else in their lives? Was it a way out for them? Was it to help them forget? No one can really answer what drives a person to take that first fix. The sadness is that they are aware of the effects by looking at the surrounding addicts. Trying drugs for some in deprived and hopeless areas may seem a way out.

When my time on the Drugs Team ended, I felt some sorrow. We had achieved a lot and were eventually recognised for our efforts and awarded a Police Commendation. I knew though that there was still such a lot to do to tackle the drug gangs, but the growing need to get officers back into uniform and on the front line saw the eventual demise of these teams.

What happened to my wall of photographs? As the operation developed, one by one, we took them down as arrests and jail sentences followed. Out of the 14 faces on my rogue's gallery, eight were convicted of dealing heroin. A total of 20 years' imprisonment was collectively given to them. In the time since, more than one of them has been released from prison and recommenced drug dealing.

I had to console myself that if our efforts had stopped one person being introduced to drugs, then it had all been truly worth it.

Chapter 6–Following the Calls

'Bravery is not the absence of fear, but action in the face of fear'

The 'Drugs Team' disbanded, 1999 saw me moving to Wakefield as a response officer. I had seen the depths of degradation a drug addict will go to; of which I will never forget and always have some empathy for.

It was with some sadness when I moved to Wakefield; it meant the end of my time at Garforth and the drugs team, but I knew it would mean a better work life balance. I had been travelling 36 miles to work and now I would be much closer. I was also ready for the change.

I worked out of Wakefield for a year before choosing to go to Ossett, a subdivision. It was a good place to work, especially as I had joined an excellent team and met a great work partner, and like all partnerships, when they work, they worked very well. Our boss there was also a decent type, so we formed a good working triangle between us.

The proof of the pudding is in the eating, they say. To us, it was in the three commendations we were awarded whilst working together. One for saving a woman who was drowning in a river. Another for stopping a man from throwing himself from a bridge and one for an off-duty violent arrest.

The job as a response officer is extremely varied and often dangerous. The College of Policing definition says:

'Assess immediate threat, harm, risk and vulnerability to determine a proportionate response in line with the law, policy and guidance to protect life and property, preserve order, prevent the commission of offences and bring offenders to justice.'

It doesn't say that you will be first on the scene, providing frontline response to some complex and often confrontational incidents. For example, there was the time when I had to attend a house fire in the early morning hours. There were people in the burning building, so my partner and I got a set of ladders and attempted to get everyone out safely.

I watched as my partner came down the ladder with a baby over his shoulders. I knew by the limpness of the body; the child wasn't alive. I remember it was dirty with the smoke and so small. I had seen the same limpness in bodies before, so knew the poor mite was dead. A sadness always comes over you when dealing with children. Such deaths shock even the most experienced police officers.

At Wakefield I also met Imran, a Special constable. We developed a good and powerful working relationship. As a special constable, Imran was one of an army of volunteers who support the police without pay. They have the same powers of arrest and search as regular officers.

For four years we were a dynamic team, and I couldn't have been more delighted when, in 2007, Imran ended up getting the 'Special Constable of the Year' award. A prestigious commendation awarded to the officer who had shown the greatest devotion to their duties. Much of it was down to the self-generated work we were doing within the local communities of Wakefield.

We were making good arrests, and he was gaining a reputation as a good Special. It really impressed his section officer with the work we were doing. What a proud moment for both of us. He was a fast learner, would always watch and listen to what I was telling him, and never tried to take the lead. It was a pleasure working with Imran and a credit for how good policing should be.

I remember a time with him when we had arrested a man, a very volatile individual who thought nothing about using his own child as a shield in the domestic incident we had been called to. He was a big lad, but it didn't stop us from getting the child out of his arms, tackling him and handcuffing him.

He was charged with a domestic assault. In Court we are waiting to see if he is going to plead guilty or not guilty. His brother, mother, and two other men come to support him. I am in the witness waiting area with the victim when she asks if she can go outside for a cup of tea. I tell her it's okay, provided she remains on call and isn't gone for too long. Off she goes with her brother and a short time later; they rush back to tell me the brother of the defendant has threatened them.

Imran and I immediately leave the room. We find the brother who'd made the threats at the top of the stairs. I tell him of the allegation and inform him he needs to leave the Court building. He initially complies and we walk him down the stairs until halfway down, and without warning, he turns around and headbutts me and kicks Imran. Now, remember, he is with two others, both well set men and they are watching us like hyenas. You can tell they are just waiting to see what we will do and are looking for weakness.

We have already overpowered the brother and handcuffed him and whilst Imran has him detained, I've had to get my baton out and make it crystal clear to the men, intervene and there will be consequences. His mother is screaming at us, and other bystanders are watching the situation unfold. It was like something out of a Wild West film, and we needed the Calvary to arrive. I call for assistance, fortunately the police station is nearby and within minutes several other officers arrived to assist us.

When the mayhem is over, the defendant in the original domestic incident pleads guilty. We are pleased because it means the victim doesn't have to go through the distressing process of giving her evidence. She thanked us for the help we had given her throughout the case, and she was allowed to leave the Court.

When I return to Wood Street Police Station, I'm instantly summonsed to the Inspector's office who informs me there has been a complaint made against Imran and myself. I ask him what it's about and he tells me it's the incident at Court on the stairs. The mother of the two brothers has complained that she's been dragged out of court by her hair and that we have assaulted her son.

Now CCTV covers the inside of all Court areas, so I tell the Inspector that a security guard witnessed the whole incident and was happy to give a statement. I wait for his reply and I'm hoping he is going to ask me the question he should have asked me first, which was "I understand you and your partner have been subjected to a violent assault, are you ok?" He doesn't. Sadly, this isn't unusual practice within the police. It just reiterated what I already knew, a complaint more often than not trumped compassion for injured colleagues.

It doesn't end there; I had to live through two days of investigation ending when the CCTV showed I never touched the mother. Police officers don't go around attacking people unless it's a life and death situation and they must defend themselves. I would never drag a woman down a set of stairs by her hair. Why then would she come out with such lies?

Easy, I was the cop who locked up her first son, and she now sees what she feels is the same cop persecuting her second son. She decides I'm going to get some pay back. Makes up a scurrilous complaint which the CCTV proves to be a downright lie. I get no apology and there is no consequence for her making this false accusation against me.

I had given the Inspector the details of the security guard who witnessed the whole incident. He said we deserved a medal for how we had handled it. He had seen the heavies with the brother and thought we were going to get badly beaten up. I asked if he would give a statement if they made any complaints. He had no issue with that at all; he was just so pleased we had dealt with it and knew he wouldn't have been able to by himself.

The consequences of us not jumping into action could have been that the men hurt innocent members of the public. It could have become a battle scene. It was already like something out of the Wild West. Only this time, the sheriffs won. It ended up that his brother also went to prison, being charged with head-butting a police officer. He was a longstanding, violent offender, and on prison licence at the time, so both of the mother's sons ended up in prison.

They didn't charge him with threatening witnesses. The victim didn't want to get involved with Court any more than was needed, and I can understand that. She is already living in fear of one brother. The last thing she needs is to fear repercussions from the other.

That story is another example of how a partnership that has a good bond works together to beat criminals. With Imran, he was a special type of person and a special officer. He was one of the few Asian lads doing the job at that time, and a real mascot for the Asian community. He used to get abuse for the sake of abuse, and we would lock people up for it. It didn't deter him one bit, and he carried on trying to bring criminals to justice.

It was in 2002 that I made my presentation to the Chief Constable. It shows I was getting pretty frustrated then with the way things were going. The mounting calls, although nothing compared to today, were constant. We felt dragged all over the place. It was just about manageable, and we could use our discretion to finalise incidents and didn't have to crime everything. Whereas now, if there is an incident regardless of whether it is or isn't a crime, it has to be recorded and a crime number provided. Even if the victim doesn't wish to prosecute or complain or if it's another person who thinks a crime has taken place. It has to be recorded. The hours it takes to complete all of this are enormous. Even then, the bureaucrats were moving in.

Ossett is a sizeable area, twenty seven miles of geographical policing with one unit on, two patrol cars if we were lucky, with a lone officer in each. It meant that we had to be really careful when we were out patrolling. If the other officer was tied up with an incident, you were on your own with no backup. The nearest help could come from a long distance away, during which time you could be badly injured or worse.

It affects the way you deal with things. It made me very mindful that if things got out of hand, I could face real danger. I would still do my job but was always aware of how close my colleagues were if I needed them. It could be scary at times; we are police officers, but by no means are we infallible. Our bones break like everyone else's.

When I worked with Paul Cooper, we had some exciting and rewarding times together. I felt unbeatable with him. We did a thorough job, but even then; the calls were becoming increasingly complex. Mobile phones had come in, so more incidents were being reported. Police cutbacks were happening. The pressure to manage the calls was increasing. As a conscientious officer, it was resonating with me.

I hated the thought that there could be some elderly or vulnerable victim that we couldn't get to because of the lack of officers available to be sent. Victims who would be frightened and waiting for a response from us, and no one could get there to deal with them.

Ironically. The anonymous letter from the 'still acting' officer I mentioned in chapter four came from his time as a response officer. In his writing, he pours out his feelings and his sadness at how the job he loved had changed. He mourns the fact that he cannot provide an example of 'good policing'. I am fortunate to have policed at a time when 'good policing' was still achievable.

He notes and I quote:

'The reality is, I'm working in an environment where the people I am arresting have more rights than I do. Their welfare gets checked every 30 minutes. They have their meals and drinks at their beck and call. Who cares if they throw those meals around their cell like an animal? We just keep them coming because what the prisoner wants, the prisoner gets. Heck, they even have their own butler (Detention Officers) who bring everything to them.'

He questions why response officers are not checked for their welfare. He screams out that he is not okay, but no one wants to listen. If I felt pressure creeping in, I can understand his sentiments of today's policing.

Once, when I was on foot beat in Wakefield City Centre, I heard the smashing of glass coming from a nearby street. This was at 1.30am. Two men had been fighting, both very well-built. One of them had head butted the window of a shop. He's obviously cut. Blood dripping from him and into his hair. I get hold of him to find out what has gone on.

It turns out that he's given the other bloke a good hiding and then to add to the fun of it, for no reason at all, he's head butted the window. He's had a good drink, as you will have guessed, and now he's going to be arrested. He realises this and grabs hold of my privates. Thankfully, my thick black jacket was long enough to be protecting me a little, but only a little. I was panicking. Any man reading this will understand the feeling.

The guy was so strong it was unbelievable. I later found out he was a slaughter man, so used to putting animals up onto hooks all the time. He treated me as if I was just another animal, ready to be lifted onto a hook.

Had another cop not been nearby, I could have been seriously injured beyond repair. The other officer struck him really hard with his baton, but it still didn't have an effect. We had to use CS spray on him before he let go of his grip. I just dropped to the floor in agony.

He was charged with assaulting a police officer but received no custodial sentence. I had to go to hospital; I was in shock. Something like that can kill a man. The Court didn't ask about my welfare, so I fully understood the anonymous writer. On so many occasions, justice isn't seen to be done. It changes your perception of life. Your 'self' talk becomes negative as you realise little, if anything is going to happen.

It leaves the victims' feeling let down by the system. We are chasing our tails. Few cases start and finish with a positive. Often, the paltry sentences or lack of prosecutions are so disheartening it's unbelievable. For me, I realised that I couldn't change things that much, even though I longed to. It was definitely the start of a great deal of frustration for me.

Einstein once wrote, "When you change the way you look at things, the things that you look at change". What he meant was if your vision of the world is one of angst, upset, and despair, then that will become your reality. I was looking at my own world through a very darkened veil and forgetting that there was so much love, hope and goodness still out there.

It's soul destroying when you feel and sense that all the reasons you joined the force for are being washed away from you. All the good things I enjoyed so much at the beginning were now different. I recognised attacking police officers wasn't viewed as that serious. There appears to be an unwritten rule that it's part of your job to get assaulted and you've just to carry on. Attacking the Crown, because that is what they are doing. We are the Queen's servants. We swear an allegiance to the Queen when we join.

It's not just about putting criminals in prison. It's about rehabilitation and consequence. Unless criminals know that there are real consequences for their actions, it becomes a chaotic situation. Once we get to the stage, where prison stops being a deterrent. Where criminals see it as an easy ride, we are lost. I've heard criminals talk about jail as a slight inconvenience to them at worst. Many prisoners with drug addictions or mental health issues often don't receive enough time and attention to even start to address their problems.

Rehabilitation is important, but it needs to commence after the prisoner has shown themselves to be capable of following the rules of society to earn privileges. They need to recognise their freedom is taken away for a reason. Understand that they don't get visits if they can't behave themselves. They shouldn't be there to come out more knowledgeable about crime than before they went in. Criminality isn't an illness and shouldn't be treated as such. We all have choices and although it may be harder to make certain choices if you have had a certain upbringing, offenders come from all social classes and 'poor' upbringing is not an excuse.

It needs to be remembered the chances and opportunities an offender will normally receive prior to them being sent to prison. They will have had restorative work. Been given warnings and cautions and non-custodial sentences. It hasn't stopped them from committing further crimes. We seem to be in a society where responsibility is passed from pillar to post. Respect for consequences and for other people has almost disappeared in certain places.

How often do you see the media showing attacks on police, attacks on society as a whole? There is no shame in selling drugs, no shame in setting light to buildings and causing thousands of pounds' worth of damage. They brag about it on social media websites. Wallowing in their fame. It shows the total disrespect for the police on reality policing programmes every day of the week, such as Road Wars.

Officers spat at, sworn at, physically abused. The playing field is unbalanced with one set of rules for offenders and another for the police officers who are just doing a day's work to keep the public safe. The increase in violence and knife crime seems to be accepted now as a norm. Where do you go from here? It's a question we all need to be asking ourselves.

When you look at what is happening, you realise why it's so important you have an excellent partner. One you can spark off. It was like that in Ossett. Paul and I were one of the best criminal catching units you will see. We used to be so charged up. If we were in a violent situation, I used to say to him, 'on my signal', re-enacting the part of the Gladiator film when he's taking his men to battle. We would laugh about it afterwards because he knew as I did, I was telling him to get ready for action. We were in for a fight.

We had some good cops at Ossett, but I could see that there was an increase in the use of violence from some of the criminals towards us. There was a policewoman I worked with, called Jackie, and we were attending a domestic violence report. I could sense immediately when this man came to the door there was going to be trouble.

At first, he wouldn't let me in, but the 999 call had come from the house, so we went inside. Now, we're talking a big bloke here, about 6'4" and 20 stone. He's mouthing off that he's going to leather me if I try to arrest him. After speaking to his wife, it was clear that he was going to have to be arrested. I had to use my CS spray on him for resisting arrest. I wasn't going to get too close to him. He made it clear he would not comply.

Then we had the trigger affect. The woman who rang 999 is screaming at me, 'why did I spray him'. All mayhem lets loose. She's 'fucking this, fucking that' at us. He's on the floor and I'm watching Jackie and this woman as he tries to crawl up the stairs. It's more than unusual for someone to do that, so I move to see what he's doing. The last thing I want is for him to get a weapon to use on us. Jackie then starts screaming and I panic. I'm thinking,' has she been knifed?' This woman is like a rabid dog, and she's bitten hard into the flesh on my partner's arm.

This is happening in a house on the border between Ossett and Horbury, and I have to shout up for assistance. We are trapped in a violent domestic situation that knows no bounds. The anger is ferocious. The bloke's still trying to climb his way up the stairs even though he can't see. He's grappling with each step, and I eventually manage to handcuff him at the top of the stairs.

Jackie is in a terrible state by this time. She's bleeding and in shock from the attack. I get the screaming banshee off her and handcuffed. I'm fortunate that the man hadn't assaulted me. He would have put me through the wall, the size of him. The woman was charged with assaulting Jackie and the case went to Crown Court. Jackie was very vocal and wanted to see her receive a prison sentence for the assault. I calmed Jackie and warned her not to hold her breath.

I think she was so angry at the growing crimes against the police that she was questioning everything about her role as a police officer. She had justification for wanting the woman punished. Her arm was still scarred, but I didn't have a good feeling about the case at all. I didn't tell Jackie that.

Next thing, just before the start of the trial, the defendant and her barrister go into a separate room. Now the Judge has already talked to the barrister, and no doubt voiced his opinion about public money being used on long drawn-out trials when someone was clearly guilty from the evidence being presented. Now

I can't prove that was the case, but then the prosecution barrister then takes Jackie into a separate room. I watch her walk out in tears and I know what's coming next. The defendant goes from a not guilty plea to a guilty plea, and a non-custodial sentence is passed down.

It affected Jackie for many months afterwards. She was very despondent. It had knocked the stuffing out of her. It's happening to officers so often that it's like a cancer spreading. The direction we are heading in now is not the right one. Unless someone comes up with more severe consequences for repeat offenders and what is causing such anger in society, nothing is going to stop that cancer.

I think anyone reading this will agree that most police officers are passionate about what they do. That was certainly the case with me. Perhaps sometimes I was too ardent about what I was doing and thinking and became too involved. I never held back from telling a senior officer when I thought something was wrong. I did it with diplomacy, but it was the right thing to do. We were out on the frontline facing the action, not them, and it's so easy to lose sight of reality sat in an office behind a desk, dealing with budgets and crime statistics.

Towards the end of 2004, my time at Wakefield was coming to an end. I had met Sarah, my future wife, and to avoid complications, I sought another posting. We had both been in other relationships when we got together, so it wasn't an easy time for either of us. We certainly hadn't planned to see each other in anything other than a professional sense, and we were extremely conscious of the hurt we could be causing.

In the force, you are often thrown together in life-threatening situations, not found in your 9 to 5 jobs. When you are spending hours and hours together in a car and having to watch each other's backs, you form attachments. You understand the pressures each of you is going through. The tension and fear when attending a violent incident or a death. The frustration you feel when you can't give your best to your job because of red tape. Only another officer understands where you are coming from, so it is easy to form a bond you wouldn't normally form.

When I first saw Sarah, I didn't think of her as a potential life partner; I wasn't attracted to her, and neither was she to me. Yes, sometimes I wished it had stayed that way, but life is more complicated than that and we ended up as a couple. That I have no regrets about. Any regrets I have are because of the suffering I caused to Sarah's boyfriend and my then partner and son we had together. I had lost nearly everything, my home, access to my boy, my beloved dog, and my status at work. You may say, deservedly so, but it's not that simple.

Sarah had broken off her engagement, which had also caused a lot of pain, and we were both in an awful place. No one leaves a long-term relationship or cancels a wedding without a lot of thought. Neither of us set out to cause so much pain, but it happened. I'm older than Sarah, and I initially thought she saw me as her dad! It was when we realised, we felt something for each other that we had to make some very difficult and painful decisions.

I generated a move to City and Holbeck division, which I will tell you about in the next chapter. It took me about four years to get work back holistically to where it was before I had made a new life with Sarah. However, as hard as it was, it was all worth it in the long run. We married five years later and are still happily together. The power of love!

Chapter 7 - Protecting the Neighbourhood

'A leader is one who knows the way, goes the way and shows the way,'

City & Holbeck, followed by Morley, were home to me for the next five years of my police career. The first 12 months I spent on response and then joined the Neighbourhood Policing Team (NPT), which took me away from front line policing.

My transfer came in 2004. It wasn't a choice I really wanted to make, but I knew things at Wakefield were becoming very difficult, and the best way to move forward was to have a fresh start at another station. Once again, I was in a strange place. My colleagues were new to me. I wasn't feeling my best. I had paid a heavy work price for commencing the relationship with Sarah, and I was in some turmoil.

It took a while, but I found my feet and it wasn't long before I got onto the NPT. By that time, I had done 12 years solid on the beat plus three years on the drugs team, so a change was needed. We had a great team at City & Holbeck, hardworking officers, along with first rate inspectors and sergeants. We had all the ducks lined up and not a lot could stop us. That status quo never normally lasted too long in the police, and this situation was to prove no different.

Contrary to popular belief, the NPT is not about sipping tea with old people, that went a long time ago and, sadly, would never return. We used to get tasks and crimes allocated to us, but we were no longer ruled by the radio and that was a welcome change for me. I was away from the escalating number of calls that were growing at an alarming rate. It would mean that I could do a lot of self-generated work again that I loved. I could get involved in neighbourhood issues and get my teeth into the genuine problems out in the community.

Whilst at City & Holbeck, I was involved in some rewarding work which sometimes involved working in the red light areas where a lot of prostitution was taking place. A self-generated operation was instigated to try to get help for the working girls whilst concentrating on the 'Curb Crawlers' who we're using their services. There were lots of problems being caused, especially in an area under the railway bridges. Complaints were being made about used condoms, needles, and syringes being discarded everywhere. It was an eerie place to be, especially at night, dark and foreboding. Victorian in its outlook. You never knew who was going to come out of the shadows.

They say that prostitution is the oldest trade in the world and I'm sure it is, but the reason the women go out and endanger themselves, night after night, is not the same today as yesteryear. Many of the women selling their bodies today are doing it to feed drug habits and to pay their pimps (pimps is slang for a person running or controlling a prostitute, taking a percentage of their earnings in return). The Victorian ladies of the night were more interested in alcohol and eking out a living to feed themselves and their families.

There is a surprising amount of work to do in an area like this. We would try to get charges brought against the pimps for overseeing prostitution or encourage the women to consider a change of lifestyle with the help of social services and drug addiction support. Often the women would refuse or be unable to change their lifestyles. If this happened and we caught them prostituting themselves again, we would look at placing bail conditions on them not to re-enter the red-light areas. This had a twofold purpose, to stop them committing further offences and try to make their own lives safer. If they were to break the conditions, then they could be arrested. We made a bit of a difference, particularly where Curb Crawlers were concerned.

What you find is many of the men looking for women in these areas are married or in good jobs, so they do not want their extracurricular activities to be known. The shame it would bring to them is as much as any threat of jail. Our efforts were succeeding; we were working and working hard, but that situation changed. I discovered years later, when I was back in the area, that the well-meaning council had made it a "safe zone", supported by a Police Commander.

This safe zone offered the prostitutes a safe area to work without fear of prosecution. The zone was an area within the red-light area we had previously policed. They now tolerated prostitution during certain times in this zone. No doubt the police hierarchy claimed they would give such an area extra police patrol, a claim that would be proved to be a lie.

How did I find this out? 10 years after my last arrest for prostitution, I was now working in a totally different police area. As we were travelling back from Leeds, my partner and I had stopped a transaction taking place in the area where prostitution had been so rife. It was around midnight, and we had seen a car pull up to a lone female walking down the street. Just as she was about to enter the car, we intervened. The woman then came out with a mountain of verbal abuse towards us. She admitted being a prostitute and accused us of stopping her earning money by interfering with this situation. She told me plainly she would report me for harassing her in the safe zone and made a note of my collar number.

Safe Zone? How can you legalise touting your body for monetary gain and putting yourself in danger at the same time? It was beyond me, but the next day I checked it out and found it was true.

Since that time, trouble has become the norm, creating havoc in the area. Prostitutes are coming from far afield, knowing they can operate there with impunity. They are fighting each other for undercutting prices. The local community is outraged. It's been on the news and in the media. Female residents fear walking near the area because of propositions being made to them.

Tragically, in this so called 'safe zone', a Polish prostitute was murdered because no one polices it anymore. That shows the changes in just ten years. All of our hard work for nothing. The women were no longer as safe. The pimps had free rein and the men could take advantage of the women with no repercussions. To know that the leaders of council and police have condoned this sickened me.

We had a great team back then, and, as I have said previously; the ducks were all in a row, but then our Sergeant and Inspector moved on. We got new replacements. It heralded the beginning of the end of my time at City & Holbeck. The new Inspector was gung-ho.

He was desperate to make a name for himself by ripping into anything and everything. During briefings, it became clear the way he wanted to operate. He would feed us details of someone who had committed a crime, but with so little descriptive information, it was almost impossible to follow up on. He would then get annoyed and demand to know who the suspect was and why we didn't recognise them. When warrants were issued for suspect's arrests, he would warn us that reporting nobody had answered the door was unacceptable. He wanted to see the suspects doors had been smashed in. The fact we needed belief to do such an act was clearly irrelevant to him.

We were in for a rough ride, and we all knew it. A short time later, one of the police community support officers had been verbally abused by an Asian male. The Inspector got a bee in his bonnet and brought it up at a briefing. He was champing at the bit, telling us he would not stand for an officer being reviled and wanted the culprit found. The general description of the suspect would have matched thousands of local males.

Sure enough, I get into work the next morning and there, sitting in my in-tray, is an arrest package with an Asian suspect's name pinned to this verbal abuse incident. I'm gob smacked. How can they have a name from three statements which have inconsistencies about what the suspect looked like? None of the officers who had given statements knew the male. Where has this name come from?

I go and see the acting Sergeant who is towing the party line in the hope he will become a full Sergeant. I ask him where the suspect's name has come from. He's hesitant but tells me that the boss just wants it doing. Then, in walks the Inspector and tells me I'm going to do it, like it or not. Now I'm due in court at 10am that morning to give evidence for an unrelated case. I inform him I can't do it until I'm back. 'Ring Court and tell them you are going to be late.' Well, it's not worth answering him. He's outright crazy if he thinks I can ring a Magistrate's Court and tell them to hold proceedings because I'm going to be late due to this.

I go to Court, then the following day I see the arrest package is still in my in-tray, but this time there is a note which says. 'You are dealing with this today.' I do some research on the 'suspect' and discover he's the brother of someone who had been convicted of the murder of a black Afro Caribbean male the year before. A group of Asian males had chased the victim down and stabbed him to death. The murder had caused a great deal of local tension at the time, some of which still existed. The brother of the suspect they have given me is in jail awaiting his appeal against the murder conviction. His family is accusing the police of racism and stitching their son up. He was one of three suspects who were found guilty of the murder.

Immediately, I am thinking, hang on, I am asked to go to the house where the murder suspect and his family live to question his brother. Now this is a young lad around 17 years old. I take some other officers with me for corroboration. I instinctively know this will not end well. I knock on the door, and it's opened by an elderly Asian lady. She sees us and immediately complains about her heart. Clutching her hand to her chest. It's clear to me what is going to happen next. I am going to be calling an ambulance.

'There is no need to worry.' I tell her. 'Please don't panic.'

I hardly get my words out when another relative comes out from another room. He is holding a phone and informs me he is recording everything and then accuses me of bullying his mother. I explain the situation and tell him I just need to talk to his brother. Then he starts.

'You're not getting in, he's not here.'

I tell him I have the power to go in if I believe his brother is in the house. Suspect and belief are the words we use when assessing our powers of arrest and search. Suspect is relatively low on that scale, whereas belief is high. I just didn't have that belief. Mum is upset and holding her heart, so I want to do the right thing and I say to him that his mum is clearly not well, and we don't want to cause any further upset or distress.

To avoid any further police visits to the house, I say to him do the right thing and get your brother to hand himself in.

I give him my contact details and ask him to get his brother to ring me and I will arrest and interview him. He takes the piece of paper, and we go back to the station. As we are waiting for the gate to open into the back yard, the Inspector comes dashing through in his car, demanding to know if we have the suspect.

'Have you got him? Is he in the back of your van?'

I tell him no, and he continues to ask if we've searched his house. Again, I say no. He then drives off quickly and I know we have not heard the last of this. We were going to get payback. I didn't care because I knew that if we had stormed into that woman's house when we had no grounds to necessitate it. I felt sure the mum would say she was having a heart attack brought on by us.

Just imagine it. The mum complains of a heart attack; the brother is recording the incident and waiting for us to do something wrong. The Community Elders would have been down at the station complaining of harassment and demanding to know the why's and wherefores. It would have been bedlam. There would have been a massive uproar from the Asian Community. Some of whom are convinced that the three lads accused of murder had been stitched up. And what evidence did I have to use such a power of search? What made me believe that the suspect was in the house? And who would support my actions? The Inspector? No way would he have supported me; he would have denied instructing me to do such an illegal act.

Two days later, I'm summonsed to the Inspector's office. He has the acting Sergeant there and asks me what the problem is on the shift. I tell him I can't see that there is a problem. He then accuses me of being the problem. I'm not dynamic enough. I then point out that my previous supervisor had given me nothing but good reports for my work over the last 16 months. He had been in his post two weeks and was saying this because, in my opinion, I hadn't complied in doing an illegal house search. That, in his mind, was a challenge to his authority. He didn't like the fact that I hadn't done what he had wanted me to do. That gets his hackles up and he shouts at me.

'Who do you think you are talking to, lad?'

I will not back down. I reply he's a bully and shouldn't be in the Police, never mind an Inspector. I will not break the law for him. I don't hold back, and I tell him my thoughts. He's furious. He snaps out that I won't be working for a bully much longer because I'm going back on patrol and being removed from the NPT team. He almost cackles as he tells me it's all been authorised by the Chief Inspector. He mocks me, then says if I want to challenge the decision I can, but nothing will change. He was sharp. He'd already sealed my fate via a high-ranking officer whom no doubt was a personal friend of his. He'd covered his bases well, but not all of them.

I make an exit out of the room. I knew I wouldn't be accountable for my actions had I stayed there. I also knew that if I'd appealed to the Chief Inspector, it wouldn't have changed a thing. Had I done so, I would have walked to his office and seen one of several posters hung on the station's walls claiming that West Yorkshire Police will not tolerate bullying or an oppressive workplace. It would be laughable if it wasn't so tragic.

I then see another colleague; Amanda, and she is in tears. She says the Inspector has also removed her from the team. The reason given to her was that she hadn't been tutoring a new recruit well enough, even though she had nothing but good reports. It turns out that Amanda had complained about the Inspector's behaviour a year ago. That time, she had got off the shift he was on, but then his move to the City & Holbeck NPT had put her back under his control.

This is not right and can't be happening. The man's out of control and a narcissist, nothing more. I decide to act, and I go to the very top. I immediately go to see the Chief Superintendent. Amanda comes with me. I apologise for bothering him but tell him I have to speak out. I open up about the search and inform him I can't hide anything I feel is criminal. I would do both of us an injustice to keep quiet and accept something that was not right. I also support Amanda, who is still extremely upset.

He invites us both to sit down to talk. I say that if I have to go back on response, then so be it, but this situation isn't right. We were fortunate because he could see through what had happened and gave us the choice of working at any of the other NPT teams situated within the Division. It was a relief to be released from there, if I'm honest.

As for the Inspector, he was precluded from promotion to Chief Inspector, certainly for that year. He did eventually make that rank before his retirement. I didn't care; I had escaped. Both of us moved to Morley, NPT. Again, we had a very good Sergeant and team. It was tremendous. We soon find our feet and are welcomed with open arms.

There were plenty of jobs to get my teeth into there. One was a man that was always driving top of the range vehicles. Range Rover Sports, Bentley Continentals, cars worth over £100.000 even in 2006. He was a known criminal and getting stopped all the time. Now, he had a driving licence and insurance because these were hire cars and he wouldn't have been able to get them without such documents.

This again shows you where the 'devil in the detail' comes into play. Officers had stopped him frequently in the past, as such vehicles were always going to bring police attention to his door. When stopped, officers checked him and the vehicles out, but everything appeared legal. The hire company that owned the vehicle would sometimes be contacted, and they would confirm he had authority to be driving the car. So, he would drive off into the sunset until the next routine stop.

I know something isn't right about this. I investigated further. I sent off his details to the Inland Revenue and DWP (Department of Works and Pensions), to see if he is working and declaring income tax. I know these vehicles can cost upwards of several thousand pounds to hire for a weekend, so he has to be getting the money from somewhere. He's been seen in several cars over the last few months.

It came back that he wasn't employed; he was out of work and claiming disability allowance. He has paid no income tax for 10 years either, so I get some of the team involved and agree the next time we see him out on the roads, we will bring him in. With the criminal intelligence we hold on him, it seems reasonable to think that the money he is using may have come from drug dealing or other criminal activity.

A couple of weeks go by and then we spot him again. This time he is in a Bentley. We are in a Mercedes van so wouldn't catch him if he made off from us, but after a poor attempt to get away; he stopped. The backseat passenger, no doubt with the drugs, tries to leg it whilst we detain the driver and front seat passenger. We arrest them for failing to stop and on suspicion of taking the vehicle without the owner's consent.

The car got recovered, and they got taken into custody at Leeds Bridewell. We have three house searches to do, One for each suspect. Prior to interviews, they are demanding to see their solicitors. It's 2am in the morning. We'd been on duty for 14 hours by now, so I suggested we bed them down and do the interviews the following morning. The Custody Inspector didn't agree and told us to crack on with things. We ended up working 25 hours straight. I had never worked that long a shift before or after.

When I got back to Morley to book off duty, I saw a Chief Inspector I knew. He was a Geordie. Used to call me Bonny Lad. So, he asks me what I'm still doing on duty. I explain and I can see he's shocked and angry as I tell him I've been on shift for 25 hours. He wanted to give me a lift home and offered, but I told him I thought I would be okay despite being absolutely drained.

The suspects had all been released on Police bail for us to conduct further enquiries. At the prime suspect's house, the hirer and driver of the Bentley, we had seized £2000 from a hidden floor safe. The car was in a compound and that gave me an excellent opportunity to get a statement from the Asian 'so called, hire company. The owner came in.

He was probably sub-leasing the car but didn't hesitate in giving me a statement. Using the previous hire agreements as backup, he gave a detailed account of the number of cars the suspect had hired from him. The amount of hire fees had come to around £14,000. We discovered how he had paid for the cars, his identity, and everything else he could tell us.

I'm convinced there has to be some money laundering offence. At this stage, I don't have a file that I can submit to CPS for advice and all I've really got is that he's spending a lot of money on cars, and it has to be coming from somewhere. By now we are weeks into this investigation, and the suspect is demanding his money back unless we can prove it has been stolen.

'You're not getting the money back. This is a complex investigation, I tell him.

I send a summary of the investigation to the Financial Investigation Team and ask them if they are interested in following it up. I'm told that their volume of work is too great and that I will have to give the suspect the money back. This didn't sit well with me. I didn't want to release anything until I felt I had looked into it thoroughly. It's a prime example of when going the extra mile and having the time to complete enquiries results in a thorough and professional investigation.

With few options left, I used my initiative and went to see a very eloquent barrister who worked for the CPS. I met with him and explained what I had. He said that in all probability the money used to hire the cars was from criminal enterprise, however, we needed an offence to hang our investigation on. That offence would be the monies he had previously defrauded from the DWP.

When searching the man's house, we seized a DWP letter that showed he owed them a considerable amount of money from fraudulently claiming benefits he was not entitled to. A check on his criminal convictions confirmed this fraud. He had been paying the debt back at just £14 a fortnight from his benefits. It would have taken him over 30 years to repay it. It was now clear that we could illustrate criminality by showing the money he is using to hire all these cars is from monies he defrauded the DWP out of.

It meant that I had to get a very detailed statement, 26 pages from the DWP outlining how he had defrauded them. The investigation that took place and what the outcome was. How long he had been claiming benefits fraudulently and any other evidence that could make a case against him.

To put the file together took me around 16 months. Why? Because nothing is simple, and everything takes time. I needed to do a lot more work with the Income Tax Office to prove he had never worked or been self-employed, so there were no earnings made by him he could have used to hire the cars.

I meet with the barrister and tell him what we have. He's pleased. We now have the evidence we need. With no explanation of how he had raised the cash and no record of any employment, the suspect was effectively a man of straw, with no visible means of income to support such a lavish lifestyle. I now suspected it was from the monies he had defrauded the DWP of which were now being used to hire the sports cars.

It's all go. We are ready to move on him. We go to his house, smash the door down, and arrest him. He's stunned, thinking he had outsmarted us again. Now, armed with good evidence of how he has defrauded the DWP, I'm able to ask him again where the money came from, if not the DWP. I got no answer, just 'no comment' as in the first interview. We then charged him with money laundering and fraud. The days of his fancy cars were gone.

Unbelievably, just before he is due to go to Crown Court, I receive a message from the CPS that the case has been discontinued. No reason was given, and I was livid. I contacted the barrister who had given me the initial advice about the proposed investigation.

He assures me it has nothing to do with me or the investigation. He simply says they had discontinued the case for "sensitive reasons". I asked him to expand, but he gave me this advice. Colin, leave this case alone. You have done nothing wrong, but you will never find out why this decision was made. Leave it alone!

I have my ideas and suspicions, but I can't say anymore because I really cannot prove anything. To me, there was a significant reason why they swept it under the carpet, but I will never know that reason. What I do know is that I spent nearly eighteen months of hard and intensive investigative work for what? It felt like nothing. To a police officer that is criminal in itself, but something we can do little about. We put our hearts and souls into good policing, attempting to make right what we know is wrong.

Can you imagine spending hundreds of hours dedicated to doing your job as it should be done, only to be told you had wasted yours and everyone else's time and efforts? You know it's through no fault of your own, but you suspect it's because of some wheeler dealing that's gone on behind the scenes over which you have no control. Demoralising is all I can say. Not everything ended like that, and I got a couple of commendations whilst on the NPT for other examples of good policing.

Morley encompasses the area of Churwell. There was a man who lived there whose house I used to pass regularly. Sometimes there would be a civilian warrant out for him for non-payment of previous Court fines. Such a warrant gave us powers of arrest and entry to a property if we believed the suspect was in there. One time, we were at his house in possession of another warrant. We were just about to smash his door in, as we had seen him sneak a look at us from his bedroom window. At the last second, he answered the door. He knew what would happen had he not.

This is 'devil in the detail' again. He comes out and slams the door quickly behind him, I'm thinking. 'Why are you so eager to get out?' I know there has to be something in there. We do not have a power of entry to his house as he is outside and now under arrest. But I wait patiently for the right time. A couple of months pass, and we are in the area again. We see him drive off from a pub carpark, his driving is erratic, so we pull him over to make sure he is not drink driving.

You must understand, we are dealing with a nasty, cunning, and clever individual. He has put a penny in his mouth to try to deceive the breath test. I make him take it out and do the test again which he passes, but I can smell cannabis on him.

A search of him and his vehicle find nothing drug related, but there is £7000 in the glove box.

He tells me it belongs to his son. I ask him if he minds me ringing his son to clarify this claim, but he refuses to give me details, why you may ask? I know he's involved in criminality, so I inform him I now have a reasonable suspicion that the cash is from criminal activity. I arrest him for money laundering, which gives me an Inspector's authority and a key to search his house. What do we find? 250 cannabis plants valued at over £200,000. All very organised with cooling fans and light/heating to keep them growing. We pick fresh growths from them as evidential exhibits and send them off for forensic analysis to see how much they would have yielded.

In the interview he's like a rattlesnake. His explanation is that the money belongs to his son, who's a famous rugby player. I ask him to give me his son's details and if he corroborates his father's story, then he is in the clear provided the money comes back clean. Now he's feeding me the line that his son has given him the cash to buy himself a car. I still can't get his son's details from him, and he's now telling me he doesn't have to give me them.

I repeatedly explain that this is an excellent opportunity for his son to confirm his explanation about the cash. The suspect hadn't been allowed any contact with him since his arrest, and any explanation given by his son would be credible. He refused to give me the information.

After consultation with CPS, we charge him with production of the 250 cannabis plants. Twelve months later, he comes to Crown Court with his son.

Of course, his son backs up the father saying that the cash was his. Now this is where a good barrister comes in. The cross-examination goes something like this:

'Now Mr Jones, if this was true, why, when the officer asked you four times in the interview to provide your son's details, did you not provide them? The officer was offering to go immediately to your son to clarify your claim.'

No explanation was forthcoming. Now he could see and feel the case was going against him. We had broken for lunch, and he was on bail, so free to come and go. He goes outside of Leeds Crown Court; my partner and I are watching him. We suspected he may not come back for the rest of the case and make off whilst he could. They make the call to go back into Court, so I inform him of this. He becomes bolshy.

'I'll go back in my time, when I'm ready.' He retorts.

Fine, but I'm not letting you out of my sight. When he realises this, he begrudgingly walks in and heads for the lift. He gets in and out of the lift several times until I tell him he's not getting out again; we are going up to the floor of the courtroom. So, with no warning, he pushes me and then smacks himself in the face, throws himself onto the floor and cries out that I've assaulted him. Now we are forced to handcuff him because he is a danger to himself and had assaulted me.

I arrest him for the assault on myself and let the prosecution barrister know what's happened. The Judge is listening to this and asks if I am injured. I'm not and don't want this to impede the case. I'm just happy that we probably stopped him from absconding the Court and justice.

He's found guilty and sentenced to two and half years for the production of cannabis. The cash is forfeited, never to be returned to him or his son. Result, top drawer, back of the net. Police 1 Criminal 0. Another drug dealer off the streets. And how did it all start? A door closed too quickly, and months of patience that paid dividends. A copper's nose and some tenacious dedication once again paid off.

There were some light-hearted times at Morley when we were not hellbent on catching criminals. Such as the time one of my colleagues placed a note in one of the PCSO's (Police Community Support Officer) trays. The message read:'Dave, can you ring DI, (DI is the abbreviation for Detective Inspector) Drayshon at Holbeck Police Station? He needs to know about a job that you went to?'

He'll not fall for that one, I'm thinking. No way. Ten minutes later, he's finished his cup of coffee, picks up the phone and rings Holbeck CID office.

'Er, yeah. They have asked me to ring a DI Drayshon. Can I speak with them please? I can't look at Dave as he patiently waits to speak to a Detective Inspector. I'm almost wetting myself with laugher, never mind dehydration!

After several minutes, the detectives in the office tell him they have no one called DI Drayshon. Without a word, he screws up the message and throws it in the bin.

Did he realise? We don't know. He didn't say a word about it.

There is no such thing as off duty when you are a police officer. I was travelling home in my car one night in the early hours. I had just finished a late shift. I'm not looking for anything, but I notice a car parked up with a heated discussion going on between the occupants. A man and a woman who are out of the car in a lay-by.

I needed to make sure everything was all right, especially as there was a bit of shouting going on. I pull up and watch what's happening. The female gets in the passenger seat of the car and is telling the male he shouldn't be driving. It's clear he's drunk; he could hardly get into the driver's seat. The car then sets off and goes through a red traffic light.

I discretely follow him and ring 999 informing the control room I'm behind this car and it's being driven erratically, and I suspect it's a drink driver. I stay behind him all the way from Morley to Stanley when the police finally stop him. He's three times over the legal limit and already disqualified from driving. I could have just ignored it, but had I done so, he could have killed himself and someone else by the way he was driving.

On average, there are 666 people killed by drink drivers each year in the UK and nearly 4000 seriously injured. When you know and see the aftermath of collisions caused by them, you realise why a police officer is never really off duty. Had he not had an argument with his partner, I would have noticed nothing and continued on my way home.

City and Holbeck, in particular Morley, proved to be a great place to work. It showed the importance of good teamwork and trust. When you have solid colleagues and good supervision, it equates to successful policing.

I made some lifelong friends there, and it was with sadness when I left. The move was for my first specialist post, the newly formed Regional Roads Crime Team. It had taken me 19 years to specialise, but this move was to be the pinnacle of my policing career.

Chapter 8-On the Road Again

'Better to be ten minutes late in the world than 30 years early in the next,'

'Regional Collaboration - Joint thinking, joint working.' Was how the new crime team was described. Officers from four police forces, West

Yorkshire, South Yorkshire, North Yorkshire and Humberside, would join to form a single unit. Their remit, to tackle serious and organised cross border criminality.

Grahame Maxwell, then Chief Constable of North Yorkshire, told The York Press that combining the strengths and skills of the four Yorkshire forces would enhance the mutual capability and capacity of forces to deal with major road crime.

Officers chosen for the new unit would be highly trained, advanced drivers with a proven record of success. They would operate in teams of eight officers, a Sergeant and an Inspector. I deemed it an honour to be selected for the team. It was an exciting opportunity for any police officer, and I knew there had been hundreds of applicants for limited posts.

Chief Inspector Mick Hunter headed up the Regional Roads Crime Team, telling the Bradford Telegraph and Argus that we were performing magnificently, a short while after its set up. Adding that the operational benefits of four forces working together couldn't be underestimated. Imagine how I felt, knowing I was one of the officers he was talking about.

The collaboration was seen to be so successful that they invited the North Yorkshire Road Crime Team to travel to the Netherlands to share knowledge and expertise with the Dutch police, who were setting up their own regional teams.

You can see then how prestigious it was to be one of the team? I had applied for several specialist posts before this one but had never been successful. After 19 years in various front-line posts, I had almost given up thinking I would ever have the opportunity to specialise. I had begun to feel disheartened when I saw an advertisement in 2008 described as a corroborative secondment of four police forces.

I had nothing to lose, so I put my hat in the ring. If successful, I knew it would involve surveillance work, helping them to stop vehicles. I would deal with organised criminals operating across borders. It would mean I could use my self-generating skills to effect arrests, so it was definitely something I knew I would thoroughly enjoy.

On the day of the interview, I met Pete England, a South Yorkshire Inspector. He and two others interviewed me at North Yorkshire Police Headquarters. A beautiful building. I was nervous. I can't pretend otherwise, but Pete told me to just be myself and tell them what I could do rather than trying to score brownie points. He put me at ease, and I did exactly what he had told me to do.

A couple of weeks later and to my absolute delight, I was notified I had been successful in the interview, but the posting was subject to me passing an advanced driver's course. I had got the job and would do everything I could to be a successful member of the team. Take any courses required of me and learn anything I needed to learn.

It was near Christmas of 2008 when I was sent to Crofton for my four-week, intensive, advanced driver training course. I knew it would not be easy. I had heard some of the instructors were notorious for punishing you if you disagreed with any of their decisions. They had a reputation of always being right; they were the trainers, and you were there to learn, not question.

This is one of the most intense driving courses most officers will face so passing it was vital. We were split into two officers per car, so whilst one of you was driving, the other was observing and there was always a trainer with you. On the second day I remember travelling eastbound on the M62 and the trainer suddenly asked us to drive the vehicle as fast as it would go. I want it flat out she said. As we had never driven at such high speeds before, I thought this an odd request to make, but we were instructed to do something, and we did it.

I recall getting the vehicle up to 147 mph and thinking, what is this exercise about? I had never before or since driven any vehicle at such a speed. The perception of how quickly we were moving on a live motorway was unnerving. I remember thinking, what are we learning about driving skills or safety here? If we were to have had a puncture, we would most certainly be seriously injured or die.

Once we had completed this task, the trainer gave a debrief that comprised her referencing how tight our hands were gripping the vehicle's steering wheel. At one point she sarcastically said my knuckles had turned white. I didn't reply as I didn't and still don't get the relevance of making two new trainees drive at those speeds on day two of the course. Maybe it was her way of testing our metal. Whatever the motivation, it was madness.

The course went relatively smoothly after that. I remained humble and kept my mouth in neutral. All I wanted to do was to learn, pass the course and start my new role with the Regional Roads Crime Team. Everything was going well, and I was looking forward to the final two days of what had been an intensive four weeks. On the Wednesday I did an overtake, one of hundreds I had done on the course, knowing that overtaking at speed was common in any traffic role. Pushing your vehicle and your driving skills to the maximum, safely, was expected every day to test your driving capabilities. I also knew full well the line between staying safe and danger was a very fine one.

Prior to overtaking I had looked and thought it was clear to go, but further down the road, a car came out of a bend. I was already committed to passing a lorry; I knew it was going to be tight to complete this overtake. I asked the instructor what she wanted me to do. 'Floor it', she shouted. I did and got back into my side of the road with about a second left, but never thought I was going to crash. The oncoming vehicle, seeing what was happening, fortunately slowed down, and this allowed us to get back into a safe position.

It had the potential to be a head on accident. The instructor got it into her head that I had forced the other car off the road. At the de-brief, I apologised and said I knew I had got it wrong, but I had not caused the other driver to leave the road. This was confirmed by my colleague in the car. Yet again, I apologised for my driving error and thought that was the end of the matter.

That evening, the trainer gave me my 'reflections' folder with her comments that I was to reflect on from the day's driving. These reflections were notes for you to debrief and give your thoughts on the day's driving. Two points in the notes were minor, but the other one was asking me to comment on the overtaking incident. She was maintaining I had forced the other driver off the road. I diplomatically disagreed and pointed out in my report that the other witness in the car also didn't see the other vehicle leave the road. I reiterated it was my error though.

Next morning, travelling to Crofton, it was snowing, so I rang the instructor to say I would be a little late, but I would still get there. No worries, she implied. Telling me we would go for a final practice drive before the main exam on the last day. The ultimate test is a pass or fail. Failure would mean I couldn't take up my new job, so I was determined to give it my all to pass. I felt I had done well on the course and there was no reason I shouldn't do the same on my final drive.

As I arrived, she was waiting for my reflections folder. She began reading my report, and I watched as her face turned to thunder. Off she marched upstairs to the Inspector, returning forty minutes later to tell me I wasn't being put forward for my test on Friday because I hadn't been "reflective enough" about my driving. Now, this was at the end of four intensive weeks of driving. I was devastated and told her it said more about her than me. I knew why she had done it. I had dared to disagree with her. She smirked and said I could appeal the decision if I wanted to, but I knew that would be a pointless exercise.

I felt humiliated as I contacted the Regional Roads Crime Team supervisor. It relieved me when Pete England told me to give it another go with a new instructor. Exhausted as I was, I wanted the new job so agreed to go back, even though I really didn't want to do another driving course.

Advanced driving is so intense you need someone supervising you who will get the best out of you. I just had to hope the new instructor could. I arrived back in the January. I saw it as a second and last roll of the dice. Fail this time, that was it. I agreed at the start of the course with the new instructor that the past was the past and I just wanted to do my course and get it finished.

Halfway through the course, the instructor requests me to go into his office, and asks me about the answer I had given to one of his questions the day before. He says, 'Yesterday at a junction, I asked you and your colleague what you could do to improve your awareness at the junction. Can you remember?' Of course, I could remember. He then reminds me I had got the answer wrong, but my colleague had got it right. I was puzzled. I hadn't given the same answer, but I had given a viable answer.

The hedgerow at that location had a hole in it, and I said you could see through it for cars coming towards the junction. 'Yes, but that was the wrong answer.' He repeated. His next comments infuriated me. It turned out; he had been discussing it with my previous instructor who had informed him she asked the same question of me, so why couldn't I remember the answer?' Now, if she had asked me that same question on my previous course, she had a much better memory than I had. Hundreds of questions were asked of us throughout that time. That was it. Why she was taking such an interest in my course, I didn't know. It was a game, and it was sick. I was done and turned to leave.

Bob Drury, another instructor, saw me leaving and stopped me. I told him what had happened, and that was it. I was going home. 'Stay there.' He ordered, and off he went. An hour passed with all sorts running through my head. My job was gone. Where would I go next, what would be thought of me by colleagues? A whole host of negative thought. Bob then reappeared, told me I would have no more trouble and to finish my course.

The pressure was off; it was like a weight had been lifted from me. I completed the last two weeks and took my final test. As I settled into my driving seat, the instructor informed me it was pass or fail, but I had leave to appeal if I disagreed with the decision. Now, remember, this was the second four-week intensive course I had taken in a matter of months. Whatever the outcome, I told him I would accept it. I was beyond arguing with anybody. I would give it my best. That was all I could do.

We went on an hour's long drive that was testing but I really enjoyed it. I knew I couldn't do anymore to pass this course. After the hour he asked me to pull up and switch off the vehicle's engine.

Silence as we sat looking at one another….'I'm pleased to tell you, you've passed.'

I was jubilant. I could have kissed the man. Well, maybe not. The pure joy and relief I felt I couldn't put into words. Elated would be an understatement. I knew I had secured my new job. The immense pressure I had been under was gone. I could move on with my career. Fulfil my ambition of being part of a specialist unit.

Once on the team, it was extremely dynamic, travelling at high speed to incidents. Dealing with criminals on the road, I felt we were like the tip of the spear. We had the assets to do the job. The fast cars, the best equipment and plenty of officers. They had taught us all the techniques to use, so we were a formidable team to come up against.

With officers from across the four forces, we were a diverse team with equally, diverse skill sets. We were all trained in surveillance, so we could assist the officers who specialised in this area of Policing. It could be that the surveillance team had been looking at a suspect for the last nine months and we would be called into the operation when the suspect's vehicle needed stopping at a specific location at a specific time.

We also linked in with an intelligence team who would supply us with details from the ANPR (Automatic Number Plate Reader) network. A good analyst would spot a stolen vehicle registration plate crime and run the number into the system. They would then clarify where that number plate was activating the ANPR cameras.

Now, sense says, that if a number plate activates cameras in Salford and then ten minutes later, the same number activates a camera in Leeds, you know there are two vehicles driving on the same registration plates. The analyst could work out which was the correct car, and which had the false plates.

They would then establish a pattern based on the times the car was in an area and work out the location it would be in at a given time. We would then wait to intercept the vehicle.

I had passed the TPAC (Tactical Pursuit and Containment) course with flying colours. Now that's also a difficult course to pass. The first few days they taught us on an airstrip. It is so dangerous to master the manoeuvre, we only went onto the roads once we had gained confidence. We could do it. Timing is crucial. You need to learn to work as a team. We were first instructed to move off as a team of three vehicles and then move up to a specified speed. You are three separate cars but must work in total unison for the exercise to be successful.

As the suspect's car is sighted, the lead Police vehicle, (vehicle one), has to place its rear bumper in front of the suspect's bonnet, a move that in training is done at up to 70 mph. The second vehicle must stay with the first vehicle's rear offside light and the third vehicle must stay on the second vehicle's rear nearside light. If vehicle one gets the wrong position, vehicle two must stay on their offside light regardless as must vehicle three. If vehicle one gets it wrong, the whole exercise fails.

The adrenaline you feel is unbelievable, and I found the best way to deal with it was to concentrate fully on my own vehicle and where I should be positioned. The most pressurised position is for the driver of vehicle one, as they must get in front of the suspect's vehicle in a manner that is so sharp it's full of risk. Everything in your senses tells you cutting into the front of a vehicle travelling at 70 mph plus is highly dangerous.

Doing this manoeuvre at such speeds and failing to box correctly could result in you ending up in your own box.

This was a totally different type of policing from what I'd been used to. On one operation we had four marked vehicles waiting to stop a vehicle for the serious and organised crime team. The suspects were involved in drug importation and, if convicted of these offences, would likely receive prison sentences of 10 years upwards. We were lying in wait for a good hour when the shout to move off came.

Within minutes, we had the subject's vehicle in sight, now travelling on a dual carriageway. I was in the lead vehicle, and we collectively boxed the suspect's vehicle in, causing it to come to an abrupt halt. Eight officers then get out of their respective vehicles and smash most of the suspect's vehicle's windows in with their batons, a distraction tactic intended to stop them swallowing sim cards or other evidence. It must have looked quite barbaric to other motorists; however, this dynamic type of stop is essential to avoid any loss of evidence or the suspect's thinking resisting arrest was an option.

The concentration needed was intense. It wound you up like a coiled spring. Over time, that has to affect your body and your mind. The other issue was that different teams use different language codes. The surveillance team had a language of their own and never mentioned street names, so trying to locate the point where you were to intercept a vehicle wasn't easy. You could have missed it by the time you realised where you were supposed to be. The expectation was you would be there and do the job. It was a real let-down if we missed a stop and let a vehicle escape.

For a time, I was acting Sergeant on the team, another steep learning curve. Managing adrenaline was the key to success. You have a mass of information coming in from all directions. You often had two radios and a mobile phone to listen to as the operation unfolded. Your driver would often travel at high speeds and it's vital you keep your cool. After a while, I got quite proficient. I learnt that there was a common theme to all the operations and the tactics available for us to stop subject vehicles. Panicking or becoming frustrated because something was going wrong just made the situation far worse.

We used to run with two vehicles that contained two officers in each one. When we stopped suspects' vehicles, it was like a military operation. The driver of the lead vehicle would remain in the car and the other three officers surrounded the suspect's vehicle.

If necessary, we would handcuff them to stop them from disposing of anything they shouldn't have and using mobile phones to alert anyone else to the stop. Once the situation was under control, one officer would go back to the police driver and provide any information they had got from the suspects. The officer in the car would then contact control, who would complete more in-depth checks on the suspects and relay any information held about the car and its occupants. This allowed the other three officers to focus completely on the suspects.

Using earpieces, the information would be passed back to the officers without alerting the suspects. An example may be that the name the driver has given is a false one and those details match someone with a distinguishing tattoo. It could also be that information is received warning us that a passenger in the car is violent and carries knives.

A lot of the times the suspects would be caught off guard. This was a new stop and search compared to what they had been used to. As time went on, some became wise and wouldn't even open the car door to you once stopped. They would hold their driving licence up to the window but have their doors locked and wouldn't voluntarily get out of their car. You then have to know what you are doing. If you have a power of search, it could mean you end up smashing a window. If you were wrong about your suspicions, then you could be in serious trouble. A complaint would be made, and discipline and civil proceedings may follow.

The same was true during a pursuit. You had to know when to abort and step away. Any pursuit is dangerous, but to go past a certain point of safety could be reckless. You must remember that all the suspect is concerned about is getting away. They think nothing of putting people's lives in danger, including their own. Driving the wrong way down a motorway, speeding through red lights and driving dangerously. These people will do anything to avoid being arrested.

I knew inside myself when the danger was tipping over the edge towards insanity. It was never going to be worth killing somebody just to catch a criminal. I would know when to say abort. It is usually down to the driver or passenger to call a stop to a pursuit.

Sometimes force control can also make that decision if they felt things were becoming too dangerous.

You realise and appreciate during the dangerous times the reason the Advanced Driving Course is so hard. You are treading a fine line all the time and have to be totally focused on the job. We aren't talking normal driving here; we are talking extremely high speeds and dangerous manoeuvres. It puts immense pressure on an officer; your entire body is tensed up during a pursuit and that puts you under a real stress. You are trained to engage in these pursuits, but you can quite easily cross a line where the consequences can be fatal.

Some younger officers can be a bit head strong but as you age, you become wiser and more experienced. I know when I was at Garforth; I had been involved in two really close shaves, near fatal accidents, and there was no way I was going to risk a third. What's the saying? Three strikes and you're out. Experience never took the passion out of my driving, but it did take the bravado out of it.

I remember one of the cars on the Regional Roads Team that was flying down the motorway from North to

West Yorkshire to urgently attend an incident. It had been raining heavily and there was standing water on the carriageways. The officers would have been travelling at over 100 miles an hour when they hit this water, aquaplaned, lost control and the car went into a spin and rolled over several times. How they got out alive was a miracle but watching the video of it shocked even me as an experienced police officer. It brought back my two close shaves and made me re-evaluate what I was doing on a daily basis.

The pressure can be immense, especially when you may have two surveillance operations on the same day. You are still coming down from the first when your adrenaline is bounced up again with the second.

For me, I had achieved a lot in my time with the team. It ticked a box of being part of a specialist department. I'd learned new skills, met new colleagues, and had absolutely no regrets. I knew I had been fortunate to get onto the team, but it wasn't all plain sailing. Some prisoners who have the opportunity to make a complaint against you will.

There was this time a suspect made a complaint against my colleagues, but as I was present at the incident, I also became involved in the investigation. I had just passed my 20 years' service, so I was entitled to be awarded my long service and good conduct medal. I was then told I wouldn't be receiving it due to the complaint.

I argued the allegation had been made after I had already reached my twenty years' service, but it didn't matter, I would not get my award whilst a complaint of any kind was being investigated. Despite my protests, I still had to wait for the investigation to be completed. The complaint took twenty three months to conclude, and I was exonerated of any wrongdoing. I was subsequently awarded the medal, but by that time it had tainted the whole event and meaning of it.

What did I learn from that? Sadly, I learned just how insignificant I was. It mattered not that I had done over 20 years in the force. They still took 23 months to complete a relatively straightforward investigation into an allegation that was unfounded. He had complained he had been man-handled too much when arrested. I recognise that such an investigation has to be conducted with utmost transparency, but for any officer, it causes an enormous amount of anguish and upset.

Such constant pressure can cause a lot of problems for officers who aren't able to handle the hours and adrenaline rushes. I was quite good at managing my stress and I left with some great memories of jobs to remember and be proud of. When I watch 'Interceptors' on TV now, I smile. I know I was part of the very first Interceptors team.

I really enjoyed the job, but there was, as there always are, some alpha males who struggled to work effectively as a team. The 'I' rather than the 'we' officers. I had a fantastic time on the team but then in 2013 we were told the Police Crime Commissioners had ordered the team to be disbanded. Whether for cost or Force politics, I don't know. I do know some officers were devastated, especially those who had waited a long time to join the team. They were heartbroken.

I was fortunate. I had been there five years and was getting ready for a change, not because of the work of which I loved. The hours, however, were killers. Sometimes 14 to 17 hour shifts, working seven days in a row with three or four days off. We were all over the place with the job and you couldn't be halfway up some motorway and then decide to call an operation off because you had done your shift. You kept going until the job was completed.

These were the jobs where we had information there were tens of thousands of pounds of drugs or some other illegal commodity in a vehicle. I would have been blue lighting all the way during the pursuit, overworked and tired, but I had to remain alert and keep my mind focused on the vehicle I was in pursuit of.

We had a lot of what we termed as 'premiership' jobs and we couldn't get it wrong. It was your reputation on the line. The other departments involved in these cases relied on us for arrests. It seemed to be non-stop, so I suppose, after five years, I was ready for a rest and change of career path. I was now in my mid 40s and although not passed it, I didn't have the same energy as when I was in my 20s.

All I had seemed to do during those years was sleep, work, sleep, work. I wouldn't see my wife for three or four days because we were both in the job. When I was at home, she would be on shifts and vice versa. It's what we signed up for, so we accepted it. After five years, I knew deep down things were starting to take their toll on me.

I was also missing the investigative side of policing I had been doing in places like Garforth, and I was looking forward to getting back to that. When you're away from local, policing in its true sense it makes you less sharp. The big issue I knew I would have to face was the explosion that had taken place with the computer systems. On the Regional Roads Crime Team, I hadn't been involved in anything but arrests. The files and paperwork had been done by others, and I knew I was now unfamiliar with the new IT systems. My investigative skills I never lost; they were too ingrained in me.

I was priming myself up for the disbandment of the team, but I would never forget the times I had on it. I remember one job at Dewsbury. It had started in

Ossett. A VW Golf R32 performance car. The driver gave us a look that I knew to be worthy of a stop. When we attempted to stop him, he sped off at high speed, in places 90 mph plus in 30 and 40 mph areas. He drove furiously and had gone through two red lights at crossroads at around 100 miles an hour.

I knew we had to abort; my colleague agreed. I was already thinking we had overstepped it a bit and should have stopped it already. If I'd had to abort when I was younger, I have to say I would have been spitting feathers, but as I matured; I realised it wasn't worth it. Pride counts for nothing if you or others are dead.

Another I knew I would always remember involved a £70,000 Range Rover. The information we got was that there was an expensive vehicle parked up in the same location where several other expensive vehicles had previously been parked and then, after two days, they disappeared. Now to an experienced police officer, what this is telling you is these vehicles have more than likely been stolen and the thieves are checking to see if they have a tracker device on them. They leave them parked up for a day or two, and if they remain there, they surmise there is no tracker on them and return to collect the vehicle.

Aware of this practice, I parked up in an unmarked car and watched the Range Rover from a distance. We knew it was stolen and on false plates, so it was just a matter of time. We sat there for a couple of hours but agreed. If no one came by a certain time, we would just recover the vehicle. Now, the adrenaline and anticipation whilst you are waiting is intense. Two hours passed and then the vehicle's hazard warning lights came on, so someone was activating the vehicle's security system from a distance. Then I see a lad get into the car and I'm annoyed because someone is chatting on our radio, and I can't alert the other car I am relying on to stop this vehicle if it tries to get out and we need to box it in.

The stolen vehicle drives off, but thankfully I managed to shout up just in time. The other police driver blocked the junction, stopping the suspect from getting out. I was in a Land Rover, so I got right behind the stolen car, leaving it with nowhere to go.

The catch to me is far more rewarding that a fast pursuit. So many tears come out of pursuits that go wrong. Getting the suspect caught in the vehicle, with no one being put in danger, or any damage to property, has to be beneficial to everyone.

Fast car pursuits may seem great when you're young and wearing rose-tinted glasses, but the adrenaline rush affects your body and your concentration, you are so hyped up. Then you have the massive fall back and the feeling of deflation that comes afterwards. It's just not good mentally or physically. You know you have to do everything by the book, make correct judgements and keep so focussed your eyes hurt, it's often not fun. It's not like in the cop films on TV, far from it.

One of the longest pursuits I was involved in went from West Yorkshire all the way down past Manchester. It was crucial when we caught up with the vehicle that we boxed them in quickly. With the intelligence we had, we knew they had a connection with Ireland and violence involving pipe bombs. In such a long pursuit your adrenaline is going all the time, you are racing through traffic, having to catch up with all the frustration of knowing they are getting further away.

When we eventually caught up to them, we put the box on. I was the lead car, so it's down to me to strike first so cars number two and three can get in the correct positions to surround and box in the suspects' car. I knew exactly where I was going to go in at, but it was at 90 mph. I remember my colleague saying, 'you don't need to take the front of his bonnet off,' because I had only left inches between us and their car. You only have one opportunity though, and if it's not done right, that's it. Game over.

When I look back now, I know I left at the right time. Had I carried on, I would have definitely been rolling the dice too many times. I wasn't reckless or anything like that but another serious accident, and that would have been it for me. I was lucky. I wasn't involved in any pursuits that ended in serious injuries or death, like some officers were.

One pursuit, carried out by North Yorkshire police, ended up with a suspect's car hitting a tree. Fortunately, the driver got out, but the car was a real mess. Normally, if you pursue a car and it hits a tree, it's a fatality. How he escaped I don't know; the driver was under the influence of drugs and also had drugs in the car. That was the reason he was trying to outrun the police.

They called me to assist. When I saw the car, I thought anyone in it had to be dead. When I saw the driver sat in the police car, my thoughts just questioned how he could still be alive. The impact had pushed the vehicle's engine back, and it was lodged inside the car itself. The fire brigade had had to cut the driver out. Miraculously, he wasn't even injured enough to require hospital treatment. If anyone had the luck of the Devil with them, he surely did that day.

If someone is injured in a pursuit, there will be an investigation, as of course, there should be. The length of the investigation can be extremely protracted and whilst its ongoing, you are likely to have been suspended from driving and at best be a passenger or office bound. Your skills will deteriorate, along with your confidence. If found guilty of dangerous driving, the consequences are serious. You could lose your job and everything you had worked for. Pension, career, reputation and a possible jail sentence. All gone because of a few seconds in a pursuit that went wrong.

The same consequences apply to any situation you find yourself in. If you go to an incident and someone is attacking you and you end up fighting for your life, you still have to justify any force you used to protect yourself. The problem with investigators or people on juries is they don't know how you felt, the adrenaline that was rushing around your body and the intensity of the situation. Without having been in that situation, it is impossible for them to appreciate it fully. In the cold light of an investigation or Court room, it's simply a case of that you should have managed your emotions.

My maturity and experience most definitely helped me avoid making the wrong decisions, but some officers on the team were young. Just like I was when I had the pursuit at Micklefield that saw me charged with driving offences. The difference was I was driving a Ford Escort. They had access to BMW vehicles twice as powerful. Like me then, they had little or no personal experience of pursuits, and a wrong choice could ruin their lives.

I remember one colleague, a great thief-taker. He had been in a pursuit and aborted it. My colleague was an experienced and competent driver, who had stopped the pursuit because he knew it was getting too dangerous. Then, half a minute later, the suspect loses control, hits a wall, and comes to an abrupt stop. He gets out of the car, runs into a local shop in Chapel Town and drops dead. There's not a mark on him, but his heart had detached itself on the impact with the wall.

The shop is owned by relatives of the suspect, so it's a frightening situation for the officer who has followed this lad into the premises and nearly gets lynched. A two-year intense investigation then takes place. Now, all this time, the officer can't drive and is under investigation until he finally gets exonerated. He's already finished mentally by that time and ends up throwing his advanced driving qualification in.

The impact it had on him, his family, and all those involved was unbelievable. It was like he was living in a pressure cooker, and the lid was about to blow. He knew he couldn't get back in a traffic car and not do his job to the best of his ability. It meant he could put back in the same situation again, and he knew he couldn't go through that or put his family through it again. To top it all off, he would have to go on a driver refresher course, having lost two years' experience as an advanced driver. The investigation cleared him of any wrongdoing, but it had been a heavy burden to pay for simply doing his job.

When the unit disbanded, I felt some sadness but also some relief that I had completed hundreds of dangerous vehicle manoeuvres without injury. Little did I know that my darkest days were waiting for me in the near future.

Chapter 9 - A Year to Forget

'You only know how strong you are when being strong is the only choice you have'

So here I am. The Regional Roads Crime Team has been disbanded and my five years in this specialist role have come to an end. What is next for me? I'm now 47 years of age. Do I go back to the beat? Which division or department will I end up in? There were so many unknowns, I definitely had concerns about my future.

I knew I had missed the investigative side of the job, so I was looking forward to potentially going back to that. That's when they offered me the Roads Crime Team at Carr Gate. The West Yorkshire equivalent of what I had been doing regionally.

At Carr Gate, I found I was working with a Sergeant I had known for years. I got on with most of the new team, so the move was relatively painless, but there was some uncertainty. Officers who had come from the Regional Team were often viewed as prima donnas, of which I certainly hadn't wanted to be.

The impression may have been that we turned up at jobs and then left them for others to pick the pieces up. Whilst that may have been the case, I never took the service we received from different divisions for granted. Yes, I was in a specialist department, but I never looked down on anyone else. I had been a front-line officer for 19 of those 25 years, so had a healthy respect for those officers.

The new role at Carr Gate wasn't as dynamic as what I had experienced on the Regional Team. I still enjoyed it, though. I was proud to say, for the first 18 months, I was one of the new team's top thief-takers because I had the grounding, knowledge, desire, and ability to do it. There were some good officers on the team who made me feel welcome to be back at West Yorkshire.

Using the previous experience, I had gained helped tremendously. I could implement what I had learned to make us a better team. We were going out, dealing with people involved with drugs supply and other illegal activities. There was some outstanding work done.

One time, I remember, we had stopped a car. The driver was clearly nervous, and I knew straight away something was going to happen, so I detained him. I found hidden in his waistband a large quantity of drugs, so we arrested him on suspicion of supplying controlled drugs. We tell him we're going to search his address once he's been booked into custody. He's nervous when he hears this and says his house key sometimes gets stuck in the old lock of his address. I ask him if he will accompany us to the house to oversee any issues with the key.

He agrees. Normally you would book a prisoner into custody and then get an Inspector's authority to search their house for further evidence (Section 18 (1) of the Police and Criminal Evidence Act). Now under Section 18 (5) of that legislation, you can conduct that search prior to going to the station if the suspect is willing to assist and their presence is necessary for the effective investigation of the offence.

So far, so good. We arrive at the property and sure enough, the suspect's door key gets stuck and won't turn the door lock. I remember him saying, 'I told you it gets stuck, didn't I?' After several minutes of trying to get the door open, we eventually force entry into the house. The door wasn't as secure as it looked. There's something about the situation that makes me think not all is what it appears. Then I find a recent utility bill in another person's name and ask the suspect who this is. He says that it's a mate who stayed with him for a few months, but why would there be a bill for the property in his mate's name?

I eventually get a contact number for his mate from our computer systems and when I speak to him on the phone, he says he owns the flat and although he knows our man's name, he says he has never lived at that address. That's why his keys don't fit the lock. He clearly lives at another address where there's likely to be more evidence. I tell him that he's got one last chance to give us his correct address and after a few seconds, he reveals where he really lives. This time his keys fit the door lock and inside the house was a combination safe which contained seven thousand pounds and more drugs.

I was pleased I utilised section 18.5. A lot of officers probably wouldn't have considered it and the suspect would have been taken straight to a police station and they may never have found the money and drugs at his real address.

My colleague didn't have this knowledge and questioned whether it was lawful to take him to the house before he had been booked into custody. I had to re-assure him it was lawful, and we had a legal power as long as the prisoner agreed to help, and his presence was necessary for the effective investigation of the offence. Working on the Regional Team had given me that experience. It was working at another level, without a doubt.

Around that time, my son Nathan joined the Special Constables. He was based at Havertop Police Station at Wakefield Police Division. He wanted to see if he would enjoy being a police officer and then he would maybe consider joining for a career. As a Special, he still had all the powers of a regular officer so he would get a good flavour of what it was like. A fantastic experience for him and he would learn a lot of new skills. I thought it would be a unique opportunity if he could work alongside me.

I asked my Sergeant if they would let Nathan come over and work with me. Initially there was some resistance but provided he did eight hours at his own division; he was then free to do his other duties elsewhere. Arrangements were then made for him to work with me. I thought it was wonderful. Now, by this time, I had moved off the road's crime team onto another team at Carr Gate.

It was early 2015 when Nathan came to work with me. We did five tours together and every time we went out together; we returned with a self-generated arrest. We covered each other's backs and worked well together. Then, on our last shift, we got the fabulous arrest of the suspects going up to the Northeast and the £40,000 of MCAT that I told you about in an earlier chapter.

I was really overjoyed; I was working with my son, and he was doing a good job. I naively thought the officers overseeing the Special constables at his division would recognise the work he was doing and give him credit for it. How wrong was I? What they actually did was to question the integrity of him working with me because I was signing some of his work assignments off as completed.

An example would be if we did a stop and search of a suspect and if Nathan hadn't already done this at his division, I would mark it off as a completed competence. Him being questioned by his Section officer affected him. He felt they were questioning him indirectly but questioning his dad directly.

As I saw it, here was an excellent PR opportunity for the police to use the unique situation of a dad and son working alongside one another in the force. It showed that the job could still be passed down a family line and that the Specials provided an essential support service for the regular officers.

It was then Nathan took a good hard look at what was happening. I remember we had a long chat, and I told him what being a police officer would mean for him. I knew he would be on the beat doing back-to-back calls, demanding shifts, front line work and getting little or no credit. I think he then looked and saw how despondent many of the younger cops at division were becoming.

The demand by that time was fast overriding supply to the point where it was just nonstop. Some months later, he came to me to tell me he had made the decision not to join the force. I was proud of him for giving it a go and making his own mind up. I knew he had gone up the mountain and seen it wasn't for him. It takes a lot to do that. Part of me was relieved. I had seen how things were changing, and I know if he had joined, he would have become extremely frustrated, as I was becoming.

I also suppose part of me didn't want him to face some of the things I had experienced. The angst and stress that went with the role. Would his marriage suffer? Would his health suffer? Would he mentally cope? I was still fairly young and fit but already had diabetes because of eating at all sorts of times, working hard and long shifts. Having suffered hundreds of assaults, I also had long term injuries to my knee and arm, and I knew only too well what the physical impact of being a police officer could be. I would have supported any decision he made, but deep down, I really didn't want him to go through all that.

Some months later, we talked about his time in the force and Nathan told me he had joined to see what police life was like. I know he enjoyed working with me, but it sickened him when I was questioned about signing his competencies off. He told me he felt it questioned me as a police officer. He didn't feel supported either and saw that officers were often seen as the guilty party. A simple mistake and your job was on the line.

Nathan gave his time freely and told me he was glad to be able to decide to get out. He also knew you now had to have a degree to really get anywhere, and that left people like me behind. People with a great deal of experience and street wise were being pushed to the wayside for people with a degree. He saw it. I had a toughness needed to police effectively that people coming straight out of university rarely possessed.

Nathan had seen the importance of being able to speak to suspects on their level. He uses the example of when he dealt with a lad who had been detained and had fought with him and his colleagues. They were taking him to the station, and he's swearing away, so they calm him down and he asks if he can go for a cigarette. He promises them he'll be no more trouble if he can just have a smoke. This is where experience comes in. They assess the situation and let him go for a smoke. He then goes into custody like a lamb. It would have been easy to take the hard line, but the trust was there. No one else got hurt fighting him and the job was done.

I asked Nathan how he had felt about working with me. He was honest and told me he had been nervous. He said it was because he had never been in a situation where he had to speak to me man to man and not son to dad. He also found it strange calling me Colin when we were dealing with people. I suppose he had only seen me in the role of dad and initially found it hard to see me switch into the role of a police officer. A serious, professional side to me he hadn't seen before.

Nathan told me he was proud to see how good I was at my job. He knew I was a good police officer, but now he knew what being a good officer entailed. He could now compare me to other officers he had worked with. I was humbled when he told me that he could see I had a real talent for police work.

It was about this time when I realised that I was having some issues with some officers on my new team. Three in particular who I will refer to as the "assassins" as they clearly had me in their sights. I did the job passionately and they didn't appear to share that same dedication. Nathan saw some of this happening. The realisation came to me when we were having a briefing, Nathan wasn't there but the MCAT job was brought up, I noticed two of the assassins sniggering when others were applauding me. I was starting to become wary. I knew I didn't have a backer on that team, and I sensed a storm was brewing, and I was going to be in the eye of it.

I'm not really sure what the catalyst of that year of hell was. Whatever the assassins' motivation was it turned into real hatred that would cause me more angst within the workplace than anything I had experienced on the outside dealing with violent criminals and horrendous crimes over the last 25 years.

Once there was a radio broadcast for observations for a vehicle, detailing there was a car with a young child in the back seat not wearing a seat belt or any other restraint. One of the assassins' exact words were, 'Fuck it, we're not looking for that, who is fucking interested in that?" I couldn't believe I was hearing this from a colleague. I had to say something, and I retorted we were speaking about a young child's safety. Again, he repeated, 'so fucking what'.

Thinking back, it probably all started with a van incident in early 2015. We were on route to Wetherby, a Sunday morning I recall. We were searching for an old lady who had been missing for several days. There were two assassins in the front and me in the back and they knew I was trying to rest before the search started. I had been up most of the night and I was exhausted. Sometimes my back plays up, so I was lying down on the back seats thinking I may get ten minutes pain relief laying straight. I need to add, police officers don't have to wear seatbelts when on duty as they are exempt.

As we exit off the motorway, we then travelled along a stretch of road that leads into Wetherby. The driver then slams the brakes on and does an emergency braking manoeuvre. I'm flung from the rear seat onto the floor of the van. I won't lie. I wanted to kill him. He had done it on purpose, and I could have been badly injured.

'You little bastard, I could knock your fucking head off.' I said in anger.

He made the excuse he had to stop suddenly because he had got too close to a car in front. I dragged myself back onto the seat and asked him where the car was. Miraculously, it had gone. I knew exactly what he'd done, and I'd been injured. I gave him the opportunity of admitting he had done it deliberately and told him if he did so that we would sort it out ourselves.

'No, no, I haven't.' he said.

He thinks he's being clever until I tell him I am going to report the incident as an injury on duty. That wipes the smirk off his face. Until then he would have had a non-blameworthy driving record. He would be seething that I had reported the incident, and it would have been recorded on his police driving record. The knives were drawn, and my back was tingling. He confronted me a couple of days later to tell me he had been called into the Inspectors office and had to explain what had happened.

I asked him what he had expected, if he got as close to a car as he says he did, in a two-tonne transit van, and had to do an emergency stop, then there was something desperately wrong with his driving. He looked straight through me. He knew what he had done but thought he would get away with it. He didn't, but it was the start of a year of hell for me.

The three assassins formed their band and set out to get me. Every day I could feel an invisible pressure around me. I felt I was walking into a den of wolves going into work. I tried to stand my ground to see where it went, but I knew it was starting to affect me. I wasn't enjoying work anymore. They had sent me to Coventry, and I had nothing to say to them, anyway.

Not only had my working relationship with these men broken down, but I was standing alone. Each week they would do something to humiliate me, hiding my uniform or other equipment. I started drinking more on my days off and was going inwards. I was struggling. They were trying to take away my dignity and crush the years I had served in the force as a commended and hardworking officer.

One day one of the assassins I was working with repeatedly asked me "Are you alright?" I certainly wasn't going to confide in him, but he asked me that same question several times, clearly delighting in the fact that he could see I was becoming mentally unwell. On the next day another assassin asked me the same question several times, again with no interest in my answer but relishing in asking me the question so many times. I knew they now knew I was struggling mentally. They were effectively using a gas lighting technique that undermines the victim's belief in themselves.

Then, one day I went into the office and at that time there's some mental health support leaflets in the room. These contained advice and support for officers struggling with their mental wellbeing. Later, during a meal break and in front of the team, one assassin holds a leaflet up and asks me if I've read it. I said no I hadn't. Well, you should give it to your wife, so she knows how to deal with you he sniggers.

I am filled with anger and humiliation but say nothing. They could sense I was getting weaker and going inwards, and that frightened me. Next day there's 12 of the leaflets in my work tray. Things heat up after that. My 'Galaxy' work phone disappears from its charger on several occasions, and I had to search for it. Sometimes I would find it in minutes, other times it took hours. My uniform repeatedly went missing and numerous derogatory comments were made about me in open forum of the other officers on the team.

I had been humiliated and physically assaulted, and they have made me suffer. Grown police officers were bullying me to the point of despair. It was affecting my home life, my character and everything I stood for. A bit of hope came when the Sergeant on the team was planning to put me forward for a commendation. It was for the many jobs I had consistently been involved in when I would always bring a decent arrest or result in. It was the work I thrived on, and I wasn't going to let the assassins stop me doing that.

I remember walking into the Sergeant's office and seeing a spoof reward and recognition form pinned to the office wall. It's full of derogatory comments about me and everyone could see and read it. That included numerous officers and supervisors from other teams. I point it out to the Sergeant who becomes uncomfortable but says nothing. I took the poster down, telling him I will not take it anymore. I'm now hitting a new low and I'm so unhappy. I don't want to come into work anymore. The treatment I am receiving at the hands of the three assassins is becoming more pressurised and I know it.

Towards the middle of 2015, I go on holiday and try to forget my work predicament. I can't and I find myself not wanting to come home. I just can't face going back to work. In my 25 years in the police, I had never felt like this before.

I go to speak to the Sergeant. I explain everything and tell him I'm not comfortable on the team. He offers me nothing but tells me if I leave, I will end up back at division. I make the big mistake of thinking I would give it another go. Why should I let them force me out? The problem was, as I've said earlier, I had no backers. Other officers on the team just didn't want to get involved and can you blame them? I would have probably been the same. You just want to go to work, do your job and go home.

The assassins obviously didn't have enough work to do or if they did, they ignored it, preferring to hide my uniform or equipment, put leaflets in my tray and pin derogatory posters up. I often wondered if they had any idea at all how they were affecting me mentally. For the first time in my career, I didn't want to come to work. What was a game to them was destroying me. How many other people suffer in a similar way?

I found some relief when I went out on duty but again, that depended on who I was with. If I was with one of the assassins, I would always be on guard because I couldn't trust any of them. I felt as though my arms were tied behind my back. Not knowing what they would do next, where they would strike. It was definitely taking its toll on my work and home life.

One time, their campaign against me reached a new height. I had been working on my computer and thought I had locked the screen. I hadn't. I'd missed the message asking me if I was sure I wanted to lock it. So, I leave the office for a short while, come back, and go back into my computer. I think nothing of it. Why would I?

A few days later, I get an e mail from an officer on another shift. He tells me he knows someone must have set me up, but he had received a homophobic email from me telling him how much I loved him. How much man love I had for him. Things couldn't get much more humiliating. The worst thing is when you know the assassin who has done it, but you can't prove or do anything about it.

I'm a police officer. I bring people to justice, but I now found myself in a position where criminal activity was going on and I could do nothing about it. I was dealing with three cowards hiding behind each other and didn't know if or when it would end.

For anyone who hasn't been through what comes down to cowardly bullying of a colleague, you perhaps won't understand the devastation I felt. It was horrific, absolutely horrific. Due to having to work in close proximity in vans a lot of the time there was no escaping it. Here I was, a dedicated and strong officer reduced to questioning everything around me, who I was, what I stood for. Three so-called professional police officers were causing me untold suffering and for what?

I was out with one assassin when a vehicle failed to stop for us. The driver abandoned the car and ran into some nearby gardens. I followed, expecting the assassin to assist with the chase. Instead, he just waited in the car whilst I'm dealing with a criminal who could be carrying a weapon or be violent. I didn't catch him so returned to my car. My 'professional' colleague is standing by the criminal's vehicle. I was angry. I asked why he hadn't helped me to be told he wasn't interested in chasing a suspect we couldn't catch. It said it all to me. This officer hated me so much he was prepared to see me harmed or worse.

I had now tolerated this for over 12 months, and it was getting like a pressure cooker that was going to explode. The feeling of isolation, the sniping and backstabbing had now got out of control. For the first time in my career, I was facing a level of hatred I hadn't felt from the hundreds of villains I'd arrested. A deep hatred, not out of anger but out of a deep loathing. Why? I can only think it's because I did my job passionately and enthusiastically which was at odds with their own work ethos.

Then came the night I made my decision; I couldn't stay on the shift with these people anymore. I was driving, and one of the assassins was in the passenger seat. He was on his phone, showing no interest in the job we were on at all. I'd pulled up and hidden our car waiting to see if a nearby stationary car may set off that could contain a male wanted for many offences.

My passenger asked what I was doing, and I explained. He continues playing a game on his mobile phone. Whilst we are waiting, I then see another car that goes so fast around a bend that its partly on the wrong side of the road. It's raining, it's dark but pedestrians are about. The driver would have most likely killed someone outright had they been crossing the road, the speed he was going.

I accelerate away and catch up with the car. It turns out the driver is just out of prison, has a bad attitude, and is swearing at me. I warn him about his behaviour and tell him I'll lock him up if he continues. I'm secretly hoping it doesn't come to that as I know full well the assassin, I'm with won't be much, if any, help. Fortunately, the lad stops mouthing off and I'm able to search him and his car, knowing he has links to drugs. Because of his earlier reckless driving, I issue him with a Section 59 warning. This is not a prosecution and basically, it's a written warning stating that if you drive similarly again in the next 12 months you may have your vehicle seized from you.

We get back to base, and we're asked by the Sergeant what results we've brought in. I state I've issued two tickets and the Section 59 warning. Immediately the assassin pipes up the warning is nothing to do with him. I remain professional but point out he was on his phone the whole time and saw nothing of what the driver was doing. He scoffs. End of, or so I think.

Some days later and more than coincidently when all of the 3 assassins are working together in a van, I'm pulled in by the Sergeant who tells me the officer I was working with when I issued the Section 59 has reported me for issuing the warning without any grounds. I have to justify my every reason for issuing a legitimate caution. I've had enough. I can't take any more of this. I tell the Sergeant I'm done. I'm not working on the shift anymore. He tells me I can't decide that and gets the other officer I was with in the office who states.

'Oh, I'd be mortified if someone gave my son such a warning for what I saw.'

I'm angry and ask him why he's comparing his son to a known drug dealer. I then point out that he was playing on his phone when the car passed us. For anyone who doesn't know, a Section 59 notice is subjective. It's down to what the officer witnesses and it's there to make the driver thinks about the way they are driving. It's a safeguard against further bad driving. So, the next thing is I am subjected to a three-month criminal investigation because I've essentially been accused of lying by a fellow officer.

I went home that night, broken. I knew I would not go back to Carr Gate. If I had done so, I would have lost both my self-control and job. The assassins were going to fit me up good and proper, and it was clear it wouldn't stop until they had done just that. They had physically assaulted me with the van incident and humiliated me in an open forum on numerous occasions. Now they were attempting to lose me my job by making serious and untrue allegations regarding my integrity. The frustration and hurt I felt was indescribable.

I thank God for what happened next. Two days into my four days off, I received a call from Carr Gate. I'd recently applied for a secondment for another job and had been successful in the interview. I grabbed it with both hands. It was a long-term investigation, away from the assassins and Carr Gate. I would have time to get my life back together again and take stock. Then, just as I had started this new role, I was asked to do one more shift at Carr Gate on Christmas Eve. A Chief Inspector ordered me to return to my old team and complete this shift. I knew it was impossible for me to work with them again and asked for consideration to work on another team for that shift. This was point blank refused.

The sinking feeling inside of me I really can't describe. After a sleepless night I went to see one of the old school cops, a Chief Superintendent at Carr Gate. I apologised and told him why I just couldn't do another shift at Carr Gate, and as I was explaining the hellish mess I was in, I broke down in tears. I was totally embarrassed and humiliated. I blurted out I would do the tour but requested I do it at Bradford. I couldn't work with them anymore. I apologised to him for breaking down. He understood and reassured me I could work that duty elsewhere. I'd found someone who showed some much needed compassion.

Breaking down in front of him, I felt stripped of everything. It was as if I was standing there naked. The assassins had taken everything from me. Fear and humiliation burned into me. I couldn't believe that three individuals had brought me to this. A once strong and unshakeable man now broken and whose dignity had been removed, layer by layer, over the last 12 months. The only sign of any hope I had was I could continue with my secondment that would take me well away from Carr Gate.

In hindsight, I now realise it nearly destroyed my relationship with Sarah as well. I'd been consumed with what was happening to me. I was giving very little to Sarah anymore. I wasn't the same person. My thoughts and life had become very dark. I knew I was mentally badly damaged after a year of hell at Carr Gate. I spent a lot of time wondering why this was happening to me and how so much hatred could thrive in a workplace. I questioned my faith and without that I would have thrown the towel in and maybe done something I would deeply regret.

Until then, I'd always dealt with things myself. My childhood memories were good, but I know I never went to my parents if I had a problem, I would sort it out by myself. I took the same route with this situation. I didn't want to put any of what I was going through onto Sarah, so withdrew from her.

The quality time we had shared disappeared, so taken up had I become in my problems. My main thoughts were how I would get through the next working week. The job and my situation became 24/7. I forgot about everything else. I could think about nothing else. My anguish totally consumed me.

Thinking back, I can see now how much it affected our marriage. It drained the goodness and quality we had in our lives. Had it been happening over a shorter period of time perhaps I could have managed it better, but day in, day out, for a year proved to have been too much. I was overthinking everything, yet not thinking about the important things in my life, Sarah, and my family!

I felt I was at sea, lost, with no one way of getting home again. Was I going to drown? Would I reach land? I went through scenario after scenario in my mind. I didn't feel safe anymore. My strength, my manhood, torn from me. My confidence was rock bottom. I was questioning the police force, the job I had been in for 25 years, when in reality it came down to three men. By that time, I had lost all sense of reality.

Worse than all I was going through, thinking and feeling, was my failure to recognise how far Sarah and I had drifted apart. We were both looking for escapes in different places. I wasn't making Sarah feel loved anymore, and I was blocking her out of how I felt about what was happening to me. All she was seeing was the man she loved, shoving her away, being upset, depressed, and refusing to let her in or help. I was also drinking a lot on my days off. I was scared, but I couldn't share it all with her. I suppose I took it for granted she would just be there.

I know now, at the six months point that I should have been less stubborn, thinking I wouldn't let them get the better of me. I should have gone then. It would have saved a lot of pain later on, but I suppose we can all say that upon reflection. I had my pride; I was strong, I wouldn't give in. I hadn't recognised what was happening with these three assassins was on a whole new level to anything I had seen or experienced before. They totally intimidated me, a feeling I will never forget.

They intended to cause me serious harm and they succeeded in their aim.

After being on the secondment for a few months, Sarah and I separated. It's as though we were no longer what we had been, united, and I guess those who had wished me harm at Carr Gate would be overjoyed at the situation. It totally blindsided me. It shouldn't have done. All the signs were there. I was just too blind to see them. But I will tell you more of that in the next chapter.

I know what I went through also affected my son Nathan, and that hurt me. He once told me he had watched as I went from a confident dad and police officer to a stressed, quiet individual who had lost all sense of fun and enjoyment in life.

Before the assassins, I would ring him and tell him about some of the stuff I had been involved in at work. We had a laugh and a joke. He will tell you. I enthused about working to him, but then something inside me changed, and Nathan could tell I wasn't the same. I didn't want to talk about my job. I had lost the sense of pride in what I did.

The good times Nathan and I had can't be taken away, though. We did some outstanding work together when he was a Special. Nathan loved being involved in what he termed as 'jobs' we rooted out'. Nathan had the same enthusiasm as I did.

The one story he always recalls, and we still laugh at today, happened one night when we were called out to search for a lady who had gone missing. Sadly, she was found deceased. Afterwards I grabbed us something to eat while we had the chance. Off I went to the fish shop whilst Nathan and some other officers waited outside. After several minutes I came out of the shop to find Nathan and the other officers had disappeared.

I radioed Nathan to ask where he'd gone. He frantically answers the radio, saying he's around the corner at a nearby pub dealing with an incident to help eject a violent male. I run round and find he's on the floor in a scuffle with a lad. I go rushing in to help him. Other officers were on the scene, but what he remembers was I was buying fish and chips whilst he was being battered!

I made up for it later when we took the suspect back to the station. He started carrying on again and attempted to headbutt an officer. Nathan was subduing him along with two other Specials. He says I was in there like a shot with a knee strike. The same one that Nathan reminded me I had used on him as a child when play fighting. He told me it had given him flashbacks!

As much as I tried to hide how I was feeling to Sarah and Nathan, he sadly saw the way I was being treated. No father wants his son to experience that. He always thought there was some jealousy about the arrests that he and I were achieving and the snide remarks about father and son going out on jobs together.

Nathan was astute and picked up on the atmosphere at Carr Gate. The assassins didn't really speak to him or me, but he knew something was wrong. He once described it to me as 'pack mentality' where no one is strong enough to stand up and say, 'Colin is a good bloke'. It is easier to be on the winning side and take the piss out of someone to make yourself feel better and stay safe from the bullies.

When your own son knows how alone you are feeling. It's heart-breaking. I was meant to be there to have his back, not the other way around. Here he was, feeling my pain and not able to help me. Is there any wonder that Nathan never joined the force? He knew how passionate I had been and how much I had changed. I think that's what hurt Nathan so much.

Did he learn anything from me? He will tell you I taught him always to be aware of his surroundings. I know we shared a lot together during his time as a Special. He told me he could tell from his experience of working with other officers that he appreciated how strong and determined I was. Nathan once told me that he was amazed at how I picked up on things he hadn't even noticed, and the respect I showed to anyone I was dealing with.

I hope and pray when Nathan reflects on his time as a Special; he remembers the good times and the enthusiasm I had for my job. I would hate to feel that my experience with the three assassins tainted that. Indeed,

I hope it taught him not to waste time on hatred and ensure you maintain healthy boundaries for yourself in such situations. He tells me he was glad he worked with me when he did. I was coming towards the end of a good career, and he saw that, perhaps before I did.

Chapter 10 - Finding Forgiveness

A new day will come, and when the sun shines it will shine out the clearer.

I started to question things more and more following the Carr Gate three. They had damaged me, of that there was no doubt. Would I ever fully recover? That was another question. Once away from them I could begin to look at things differently. Over the last several years, I had been thinking about faith. I guess if somebody had asked me years earlier do I believe there is a God, I would have said maybe. That's despite the angst and turmoil I was seeing every week in the police, I knew these were mans' actions, not Gods.

Was I looking for something? I expect so. Was I looking to rebuild back the belief in myself through God? I don't know. I know I felt some peace and was ready to take back control of all that I had lost. I questioned the cliché 'things happen for a reason'. Would I have changed my spiritual direction in life, had the events at Carr Gate not happened? I can't answer that, but I can say I am thankful to have found faith and in doing so, forgive the people who had hurt me so badly.

I look back at Carr Gate. Whatever reason they had for choosing me as their target, I forgive them. I will never forget what they put me through, but I will not let it move forward with me. As Nelson Mandela said of his captors on being released after years of imprisonment, 'If I do not forgive them, I may as well turn back around and return to my cell '.

Forgiveness doesn't come instantaneously. It took a lot of soul searching. Another man who inspired me by choosing to forgive rather than being consumed by hatred was the son of the first Yorkshire Ripper victim, he had recognised the need to forgive Peter Sutcliffe so that he could be released from the trauma and hell he had faced in the aftermath of his mother's murder. It takes so much courage to forgive someone who has hurt you so much, but in doing so it stops you from becoming the next victim and you then become the victor.

I'm glad I chose to walk the path that I did because I am sure the other path would have led to potential self-harm and premature death. I know that may sound dramatic, but I was at rock bottom, the tunnel I had entered was a long and dark one. Now I could see some flicker of light at the end of it.

In the Bible, Psalm 29:11 says:

'Forgiveness is about letting go of the anger and your desire for revenge. Realise you are powerless without God's strength. God does not ask you to do something without giving you his strength and power to do it.'

I did find, and have found since, that being willing to forgive puts me back in control. It takes the victim label away and gives me strength. I don't want or need a life of bitterness. Suddenly the pressure was off of me. I didn't have to face the storm alone; the weight of pain had gone. Holistically, my compass had moved massively. It humbled me by showing me what was important in life and what wasn't.

I was now moving on from Carr Gate, a blessing in itself. I hadn't given myself emotionally to Sarah. I had closed off, and I knew that hurt her. I know she was sad and upset to see me going through what I went through. My nature of dealing with things is to go inward and quiet. I was always loving and affectionate, but marriage is more than that. It's about sharing each other's burdens as well as enjoying each other's happiness. I had forgotten that. I was consumed by my own inner turmoil and for a time nothing else entered my mind.

Sarah was also a police officer and although she knew the stress that comes with the job, I didn't feel she understood the internal pressure when the people who you think have your back are the very ones stabbing you in it. Sarah will say she hasn't been through what I have been through work wise, but she knew that one person trying to deal with it couldn't. She once called it a beast, and she was right. I couldn't tackle them on my own.

As things got worse, Sarah began to feel more isolated. She knew I was fighting to keep my head above water and saw me drowning but I wouldn't let her in to save me. I am a really deep thinker and chew things over and over. Sarah is the opposite; she lives in the moment.

Maybe I should have, but I didn't see how upset Sarah was becoming too. She told me later how much she used to worry about me, especially when I was at work. She recognised that every time it came to the end of my rest days, and I had to return to Carr Gate, my whole demeanour changed. If I look at it now, I know that we were both living the hell, but in different ways and neither of us were talking to one another about it.

I was at the point of having no self-belief. Sarah later told me that I was a shadow of the man she married. The situation had started out of hatred which in turn produced more hatred, a pressure cooker of negative energies waiting to blow.

In relation to our marriage, the fun had gone. We were worrying about each other but not explaining our feelings to one other. We were still physically living together but spiritually moving apart. I began drinking alcohol a lot on my rest days to try and forget about work. Sarah began exercising excessively. It worried me because I knew she had struggled with this in the past. In any emotional crisis, she would just run and run and run. It was her coping mechanism.

Then, suddenly she was gone, she had left. I had started my secondment by now and didn't expect it at all. Part of me was perhaps just blind to how much we had grown apart.

Sarah will tell you, she was lost and not thinking straight. I know she had always put me first, probably to the detriment of herself, but she was pushed to the brink, I suppose. I didn't see it then. We were both in fragile mental states. How fragile neither of us really knew.

I had lost a lot of my self-esteem and confidence at Carr Gate, so I was trying to find it again in the new role. A stressful job, dealing with a large Gypsy operation. I will come to that later, but I was putting my all into it and not really paying attention to much else. The last 15 months were now coming home to roost.

One evening Sarah and I had a long talk, and during it I realised we had lost one another. It was clear we were going in different ways. The sixth sense that had protected me so many times from imminent danger was now telling me your soulmate is leaving you. She left the house. I was on my own with the negative thoughts of how much of a failure I was. At times I thought it was karma catching up with me, for all the wrongs I had done in the past. A once proud officer and husband now felt worthless, both aspects of my life were in tatters.

Everything had been stripped from me, I felt deeply humiliated and lost. I felt like the 'Gladiator', who lost his wife and everything else. But I wasn't Gladiator. I may have thought I was at one time, but such preconceptions about my prowess on the battlefield had disappeared a long time before. I realised I had lost hope and after losing hope I was heading backwards into an abyss.

After weeks of this negative and torturous cycle, I walked out of our home for one last time. My thoughts were telling me I was a failure, an embarrassment, and nothing would make this situation better. Time to do the honourable thing and end the hellish thoughts I was now living. I couldn't sleep for more than a few hours a night. The last 15 months had caused me to become mentally unwell and I would subsequently be diagnosed with clinical depression. At the time I just thought I was going mad and could see no goodness in life. If you had asked me where God was at this time, I would have said I really didn't know.

As I walked out of the house, I felt I was on autopilot. It was like I was acting outside of my body, almost like a dream. Just as I was leaving, I saw Junior, my beloved dog and faithful friend, looking at me. Looking into his eyes, I saw a deep understanding. He loved me unconditionally. If I left, who would look after him? How long would he be here without food and help? That was my moment of realisation what impact it would have on others. Not only for Junior, but to my son and others who loved and cared for me.

The spiritual energy I felt in that at moment was incredible. I liken it to a boxing match. I had been in the ring for 26 years and taken and given some extremely strong punches. The last 15 months had seen me get hit too hard, too many times, and I had been put on the canvas for the first time. I didn't know how it was going to end, but I knew I couldn't go back down on the canvas again. That would be the end. For now, I was holding onto the ropes until I could hopefully recover.

I knew I was very unwell, and I requested an urgent appointment to see my doctor who referred me to a mental health specialist. Shortly afterwards I was assessed to ensure I wouldn't harm myself. I dug deep and threw myself into the complex investigation I was now involved in. Fortunately, at the time I didn't know the many battles that still lay ahead of me with the police and how they would mismanage my mental illness. For now, though I was on my feet, albeit extremely weakened and battered by the storm.

I remember cleaning the kitchen floor and speaking spiritually to my mum. Don't worry mum, I won't harm myself I promised her. This was another defining moment when I knew I would recover something from this hell I was living. Weeks turned into months and Sarah eventually returned home. We still needed one another. There was a deep love between us and although we had lost our way, what we had was worth saving.

It wasn't easy for either of us at first. Sarah couldn't forgive herself for leaving and adding to my hurt. We both had a lot of forgiving to do. Sarah told me she never wanted to be away. She wanted to be with me and Junior. We all do things we later regret, but the important thing is to understand why we do them. I understood that fully.

Even when she returned, I knew we weren't holistically balanced. Sarah wasn't herself mentally. She had tried hard to overcome her problems, stop the obsessive exercising, and I knew she, like I did, desperately wanted us to get back to where we had been before Carr Gate. When she needed me, I hadn't been there. I had been nowhere apart from adrift in my own mind.

Perhaps she had needed space to work through things, and perhaps I also needed that space. Neither of us found it easy, but we both knew, before all of this, that we had been very strong even though we are totally opposites. What's the saying opposites attract? We had been through so much together. When we first met, our love was tested to its limits, so we knew it was strong. Would it be strong enough to survive this, though?

Starting again took a lot of faith and compassion. I know Sarah looks to herself for blame, I don't. How did we overcome our turmoil? My faith had humbled me a lot, made me see things in a different light. Would we have survived had that not been the case? Who knows? We had a deep love, of that there was no doubt. Sarah in time also found faith, so this in turn enriched our relationship considerably.

They always say, what doesn't kill you makes you stronger. Well, it could have killed me, but ultimately, it strengthened us to a higher level than we could have previously imagined. I liken our relationship to that of a once beautiful house, now in ruins. We had to rebuild but this time the foundations had to be stronger. God was mixed into those new foundations and strengthened them immeasurably.

I think it still surprises Sarah that we have repaired and recovered so strongly, but it doesn't surprise me. Our time apart brought us both to our senses. Showed us both what was important to us. We have both changed as people and for the better.

We both sought release in different ways. I suppose mine came from becoming too intense with work. Sarah's came from taking control through needless exercise, the only way she knew how. When we reunited, we both had to refocus and, in doing so, we both found ourselves again.

Sarah understood better than I ever did that the police force had changed so much. Someone like me, from the old school, didn't really fit in anymore. I had become a round peg in a square hole. My work ethic didn't seem to sit well anymore with modern policing, and certainly not that with those officers who had caused me harm. Had it done so, perhaps none of this would have happened, but then I wouldn't have found my faith and that, to me, is priceless.

If you ask Sarah today where we are, she will tell you we are stronger than we have ever been. I don't take things so much to heart. We talk a lot and never take what we have for granted. We have both experienced deep pains, but I wonder if we would have understood each other so well had we not gone through this storm?

We laugh again. We don't forget the pain, but we understand it. Sarah has never experienced the issues I have had at work, but she knows me well enough to recognise how much it affected us. Don't misunderstand me, I don't put everything down to Carr Gate, the way we handled things, myself in particular, could have been better. I am a firm believer, however, that life is about learning, and learning to forgive is what life is about. Sarah and I have found ourselves; we are now at total peace with one another.

We have since faced other difficulties including a devastating loss and trauma. It tested us but with our faith and strength we got through things. This time Sarah didn't seek escape in exercise and eating and I didn't isolate myself like before. We communicated and supported each other.

Sarah puts it greatly. She says that our seesaw was out of kilter and needed to be rebalanced. Everything that happened balanced it. Our love for each other is stronger than ever and I know nothing, or no one, can change that. Only Sarah and I. There is no blame between us, no mistrust or desire for vengeance. That has all gone. We have grown through this and will continue to grow.

Chapter 11 - Gypsy Valley

'Attention to detail is the foundation of good detective work'

I have mentioned the Gypsy operation several times. This is the story. I left Carr Gate, being determined I would never go back. There was too much hatred and bad memories of the place for me to be confident I could return there safely. I firmly believe that if I had of returned my policing career wouldn't have survived.

I was at a crossroads. The secondment was my saving grace. Whilst I admit, a part of me saw it as salvation, I really wanted to do this job as it involved working with vehicles and organised car crime, and I had a feeling that it would be an interesting investigation. The pitting of wits and utilisation of investigative skills really appealed to me.

It turned out it was meant to be. The phone call telling me I had the secondment was a lifesaver for me. I don't deny that. I started in the December. It turned out to be a massive investigation. It concerned the theft of Ford Transit vans. Now, when you consider at that time 40% of all vehicles stolen in the Yorkshire and Humber areas were Ford Transits, you see the size of the problem.

Why? The vans had an Achilles's heel if made during a certain time period. The Achilles heel being that the ignition key Ford had manufactured for the vans could easily be replicated. The ignition system would pick up that the code on a duplicate key was different, but a de-coder sold openly on the internet market could bypass the vehicle's immobiliser system. Provided there was no other security device fitted to the van, you could be in and away with it in three minutes.

So serious was the issue. It left Police forces with a dilemma where were these vehicles going to. The vans were disappearing, never to be seen again, but they were going somewhere, that was for sure.

Civilian researchers spent many hours trying to figure it out. They began by inputting the stolen vehicles registration numbers into the ANPR systems and picking out any that had a unique livery or distinctive features.

Next, they would look at all transit vans that had passed other locations after the original thefts had taken place, the suspicion being that the stolen vehicles were being placed on false registration plates. They would then look at these pictures for the unique livery on the stolen vehicles and were able to link those to a van now being driven with a cloned registration plate. The work was painstaking, but vital to shed any light on the whereabouts of the stolen vans. Imagine, we are talking about hundreds and hundreds of vans to look at, hoping to find something unique about them.

It was like looking for a needle in a haystack to find these vans, but the researchers eventually matched up about 70 stolen vehicles. It was then ascertained that 70% of them were being taken over to the Oldham/Manchester border. The intelligence suggested that they were heading towards the Lancashire area.

The research continued, but you are now talking about an area of around 100 miles where these vans could be taken. It was like searching the Bermuda Triangle, fathoming how these transit vans were disappearing from view after activating certain cameras. When looking closer at the geographical areas, we realised our likely suspects lived within that triangle. This family was notorious and had an established scrap yard business.

When I say scrap yards, I'm not talking about a dirty playing field sized yard you are probably imagining. I'm talking about an extremely organised and enormously big scrapyard. So large, the owners sizeable stone built detached house sat within it. In a good postcode, the house would be worth around £3.5 million. The finest Italian leather and marble decorated the inside of the house, whilst two twelve-foot-high stone statue lions stood guard at either side of the house's security gates.

We were aware of the family; we knew them through the previous mayhem they had caused in the local area. Criminality, threats and antisocial behaviour. They were very well known to the police.

The other evidence that indicated we were on the right tracks, other than their location, came down to a suspect who was a functioning heroin addict who lived in Leeds. He had stolen a transit van in Leeds and crashed it within two miles of the scrapyard's location. That gave us some feeling of certainty that something would be found in the yard.

Our force linked in with Lancashire and three other Police forces to combine the resources of over 300 officers, so you can imagine how big an operation it was.

We knew Lancashire police had executed a search warrant at the yard some 18 months earlier but had found nothing of evidential value. Then again, in a yard the size of five football pitches, with only a handful of officers, it's easy to miss things.

Prior to the raid a massive briefing takes place involving hundreds of officers. My colleague and I, who are running the operation, stay in an office hub, monitoring the information that is being relayed back from the officers who are now entering the scrap yard. In the first hour we hear the first piece of stolen car part has been recovered, which then turns into hundreds more throughout the day.

It's clear we have struck it big. During the week long operation thousands of stolen vehicle parts that consisted of engines, panels and every other saleable part are recovered. It becomes obvious to us; these vans are being stolen to be broken down into their component parts and then sold on to maximise profits.

So big was the search, it took the dedicated search teams five full days to complete it. Over 30,000 exhibits were recovered that included thousands of vehicles panels and engines. A huge enquiry in anybody's book. The prime suspects, who were as crafty as rattlesnakes, lived on the outskirts of a small village where they had lived for seventeen years and knew everyone and everything. Nothing got past them. Now, imagine a small army of police vans and cars coming down the road. They will surely be seen, and they were.

A likely tip off resulted in the suspects rushing into a vehicle, and off they fled, followed by another car, its passenger door repeatedly flapping open and shut, driven by somebody with a suspected commodity in it. It may have been drugs or a gun, we don't know, but it's all captured on the yards CCTV that the suspects have tried to erase electronically after they had absconded but had failed to wipe out. They went off in one direction and thirty seconds later; the first Police vehicles entered the yard. The only people still on the premises were several workers.

Recovering the thousands of stolen vehicle parts from the yard was a herculean task and we would usually use a local recovery company to do this. This was not possible on this operation. Why? We were advised by all the local recovery companies that they were receiving threats, telling them their premises would be burned down if they went into the yard. Now when you think, some of the men running these recovery firms are tough guys, definitely not shrinking violets, it tells you a lot. They were clear about what could happen if they helped us move the stuff.

One man told us he wasn't worried about himself, but his workers. He said the suspects knew where they drank, and they would look to do them some harm. We understood perfectly and wouldn't ask them to do anything that could put them in danger. So, it's up to us to move the parts. We had to take them to a covert location using police low-loaders from across the regions.

We've now realised this is a much bigger operation than anyone thought. I'm thinking it's going to need a large team to handle this, and I'll be on it with numerous other officers. It was clear from the search results; it was an investigation that would take years to complete, and it did. Not in the way I expected, though.

Initially, it was hailed an enormous success with a police boss appearing on national TV championing the operation, holding up pieces of recovered vehicle parts. Explaining how seriously such crimes are taken and how good the police are at doing their job. But, as soon as the furore had died down, the staffing left to investigate matters was my colleague Mark, someone I had worked with at Garforth, a part-time officer from another force and myself. Full stop. That was it.

I knew we were going to be up against it. We were, effectively, two and half officers, left to bring convictions against suspects who had been getting away with organised criminality for years. It was going to take every police investigative skill we had and hundreds of hours of work to bring them to justice.

Mark did some research on the suspects and its then we got a flavour of who we were dealing with. The suspect's solicitor emailed him informing us that the owners of the yard were on holiday but understood we had carried a raid out at their yard. He purported to be there to help us with enquires on behalf of his clients. Mark sent an email back informing him. Yes, they were going to be arrested in connection with the offence of conspiracy to steal motor vehicles. Please could they present themselves at a police station to be arrested by appointment?

Nothing wrong with that other than when Mark sent the reply. He forgot it was on an email with his mobile number on, usually an accepted practice. Unfortunately, one of the suspects who got hold of the number rang up, threatening us. Not once, not twice, but over a hundred times over the next two days. We were going to be sued; we had taken this and that illegally. Our warrant wasn't legal. On and on it went. He laid claim to at least 18 pieces of property, all of which I noted down that we had supposedly "stolen" from him.

The calls got to the stage where Mark had to change his work's mobile number because the suspect would not stop ringing him with menacing, intimidating threats. Neither Mark nor I were surprised at the volume of calls. We knew what it was like to deal with some gypsies.

When I had worked with John on the drugs team, he told me of a time when he was called to a firearms incident. It turned out to be a dispute between two gypsy families from different sides of the track. One man broke into the other's house armed with a shotgun whilst the other was still in bed with his wife, but before he could fire, the one in bed pulled a rifle from under the bedclothes and shot first.

It showed us how ruthless the people we were dealing with could be. He also told me of a time when he arrested a gypsy who was around 25 with a full beard but tried to say he was under ten to avoid arrest. We laughed at that one, but constant harassment over the phone isn't and wasn't funny.

Some days later, the suspects hand themselves in, not together but separately. I will later refer to them as Fred and Jeanie. The male strolls into the police station first to find out what we know. He looked insignificant, but having researched him, I was only too aware that this man was anything but that.

He was an organised and successful criminal who would use sickening violence to run his criminal empire. A man who rose at 6am in the morning and worked tirelessly until 11pm. He used neither alcohol or drugs and was very passionate in what he did. After he had been arrested and booked into custody a lengthy interview then took place with him and his solicitor and it went something along these lines:

'I'm a simple man officer. Last year they made me a bankrupt after I got out of prison and I'm on a seven-year prison licence. I can't do anything wrong officer, but I am making a complaint about you and your colleagues because this isn't going to do my reputation any good.'

He says all of this with a straight face. So here is a 'simple' man who continues to say:

'I look after the 147 horses and donkeys that are in the yard. If you look at the bankruptcy files, I sold all of that property for a pound to my wife. My wife owns the scrap yard officer, so you better speak to her because I don't know anything about any stolen property.'

Okay, I'm thinking. Checks did reveal that he has indeed previously sold the scrap yard to his wife for the grand total of a pound. He then tells us a date and time when his wife will come in for an interview. Indirectly suggesting he is going to be in control, not us. He's then given Police bail and as he's leaving, he looks straight through me and says: 'You are going to have to do your homework on this one son.'

He was right; I was going to have to do my homework and more. I knew this was going to be a massive challenge, but one I would step up to. Mark and I were going to have to utilise every ounce of the investigative skills we had gained from nearly 60 years of Policing to get this case solved.

Seven days go by. Then, as agreed, his wife turns up. We arrest her, and before we begin the interview, she places some documentation on the table.

'Can I just ask officer before you question me. I'm led to believe that 99% of the property you say was stolen was recovered from my yard in this section here?'

She points to the paper. I agree with her; she is right; it was. Next, she hands me a lease, which just happens to be for the part of the land where we had recovered 99% of the stolen goods. Now this turns out to be leased to a man called Martin O'Connor. She tells us he's a traveller who has paid her £400 a month rent for that area of the scrap yard. He had paid the rent in cash, so there were no receipts. She then says:

'I know you'll think I'm lying officer, but I've also got an accredited solicitor who will swear on an affidavit that he was present when Mr O'Conner signed the agreement, countersigned by the solicitor and myself. That's who trades off that land. Now I've been told there was a lot of stolen property that's been found. All I can say is what Mr O'Conner did is his business, not mine.'

I'm speechless. She proclaims she never gave Martin O'Connor permission to sell stolen property and that she wouldn't have him on her land if she knew that's what he was doing. She also has a solicitor who will corroborate this story.

What can you say to something like that? I knew it would take some refuting.

The next major step was for us to identify every item recovered from the scrap yard by the search teams. They had done a good job, seizing the vast majority of stolen property from the yard. It had been down to the sheer number of officers working on the job. Lancashire police had previously gone in with just one team made up of five officers, obviously they had stood no chance. It would have been like looking for a needle in a haystack to them, whereas our operation had thrown everything at it, but now we had to try to identify every single piece of property that had been recovered.

Arriving at the yard where the parts were being kept, all I could see was a landscape full of bits of vehicles, thousands of them. My heart sank. How were we going to sort it out? Where did we start? There had been so much recovered, no statements had been taken, only notes of what the officers had recovered.

It took three weeks of backbiting amongst police forces before West Yorkshire agreed to provide two of the original vehicle examiners who had been there on the day of the operation. Overtime would be paid plus lodgings for a week. It took us five solid days to go through everything. Some civilian vehicle inspectors who were there on the day also came to help us. Without such specialists we would have never been able to say which stolen parts belonged to what vehicles.

The vehicle inspectors were experts at knowing where to find hidden identifying numbers on parts we wouldn't have any idea about. So, we completed a mammoth task in a week. I started a logbook and noted down every detail about the stolen items. When it was stolen, why the examiners had said it was stolen, where in the yard it was seized, and the tag number given to it.

Bit by bit, like worker ants, we went through every piece. Identifying, tagging, recording, it seemed endless, tedious work. There were hundreds of thousands of pounds worth of spare parts from hundreds of vehicles. Total profit for the suspects.

It wasn't long before we passed the one million pounds mark of recovered stolen property. I remember thinking that even if there's ten million pounds worth the suspects have a solid defence with Martin O'Connor in the frame. The yard ended up looking like a vast jigsaw puzzle, with pieces being fitted together to form vehicles. 30 foot high ladders had to be used so that photographers could take aerial shots to illustrate the scene.

What had seemed like an impossible task at the beginning was starting to come together bit by bit. All down to the meticulous work carried out by the vehicle inspectors in what I add was foul weather on a cold, miserable week in March. It was freezing, but we had a job to do before we could move onto the next stage. Then, in the middle of the week we got a massive break. I had noticed the plastic police tags attached to the recovered items but then I also saw written in permanent ink, what appeared to be coded numbers on most of the parts.

Let's say it was a Volkswagen part, it would read VW 235 or an Audi, A 674. I'm puzzled and ask the examiners why they had put these numbers on the parts. It becomes clear, the plastic tags are theirs but not the other writing. This had already been on the panels when they were recovered, they inform me. It was a eureka moment. I knew somewhere in the mass of seized paperwork or on a computer, there must be a ledger of some sort.

We knew in the way the suspects kept the yard so immaculate we were dealing with very organised and skilled people. There would be records and we would have to find them. There was still a colossal amount of work to do. Statements had to be taken from people up and down the country whose vehicles had been stolen. Before all of that I knew we had to find the ledger. What we had was millions of pounds in stolen vehicle parts, but nothing that refuted the suspect's defence.

It would all come back to Martin O'Connor renting the land. Nothing to do with the suspects. We had made a lot of enquires to find the missing renter but found nothing. Plenty of Martin O'Connor's', but we were chasing shadows. I knew it didn't matter how many statements we collected; nothing would progress the case without the discovery of the ledger showing that our suspects were involved in the thefts.

Back at the office we searched the mountain of paperwork that had been seized for over 20 hours and then came across two books. It was a genuine breakthrough. I was elated. In the books were records of parts sold. It was like finding a map leading to the buried treasure. Entries would list the part, the number assigned to the part, when it had been sold and the price it sold for. So, it might read:

F86 Left wing mirror, Ford Transit, SOLD

On every receipt, the female suspect, who was now running the business, had a note of the purchaser. It was like gold dust to us. The suspect, being meticulous as she was, had kept excellent records of all transactions to do with the parts, down to the attaching of Visa receipts onto the paperwork. The buyer received a copy when the parts were sent to them.

Fabulous, we now had a buyer's name, address and bank account where the money to pay for the parts went. Most of the buyers had purchased the parts in good faith, paying a reasonable retail price. Now, we could trace and obtain statements from them, identify the property they had purchased was stolen and damningly for Jeanie, proof she had sold them the parts and then put the money into her own bank account.

We also discovered she was running another business in the same yard called "Jeanie's Money". It was a separate enterprise. If someone brought scrap in, she would pay them with a cheque. It is criminal offence to pay a customer in cash for any scrap they have sold. The customers then trotted off to "Jeanie's money shop" situated within the scrap yard and exchanged the cheque for cash. Jeanie then ripped the cheque up.

Whilst all of this is going on, the couple are on bail, still running the business, totally unaware of our findings. Six months later, she is back at the police station, and we present her with the evidence, drip feeding it, bit by bit. Horrified, she knew the game was up.

We also had her fingerprints on some of the receipts. The ledger was in her writing. We had identified over a dozen items of stolen property that she had sold, and the part numbers fitted in with the gaps we had when we had been sifting through the mountain of stolen car parts. She had nowhere to run.

Her reaction to further questioning was 'no comment' to each and every question. It didn't matter, we had the evidence we needed. Her husband, we didn't quite have. We had arrested six of the workers on the day of the operation. They were absolutely petrified of giving any statements to us but what they had done, inadvertently, totally unaware of what Fred had told us, was to break the pretence that all he did was look after the livestock in the yard. Fred was the one who interviewed and employed them. It also became clear it was Fred who paid them and ran the yard. All roads led back to Fred.

CCTV footage damned him further. It showed his son and him putting chains around an engine to move it and him then selling it to a male customer. It wasn't a stolen engine but had been sold by Fred, so we got a statement from the buyer. He confirmed he had bought the engine from Fred. The links were now forming, and it was becoming clear he was not the sleeping partner he was claiming to be.

We still didn't have sufficient evidence to pinpoint how he was linked with the 'parts' operation. So, when we interviewed him again, I took my pad with the notes of everything he had claimed some eight months before when my colleague had to change his phone number.

We got the stock answer 'no comment' at first. He was acting belligerent by then. We had tied Jeanie up in knots, and he knew it. The problem was, she came from a big gypsy family. He was more than aware they would be very upset. He had shit in his own nest and was leaving Jeanie to take the rap. This is his wife who had given him four children.

He continues to 'no comment' all questions put to him, so I decide to try another tack. I ask him if he can remember how upset he was when we he learned that we had executed the search warrant. He immediately starts shouting and going off down the same track. He rattles on for a good five minutes about how he is still challenging the validity of the warrant and how we had no authority to take anything from the yard. I highlight how in his previous interview he was very upset at losing some items he claimed was his personal property.

One item was a golf buggy. I showed him a picture of it and he became irate telling me it was his and where he had bought it. 'When and from whom'? I ask him. A man he says. I inform him it was stolen. He tries to convince me he paid good money for it but won't tell me who he purchased it from. We then move onto a caravan that was situated in the scrap yard; electricity supplied to it by his own house. He tells me it had been left to be auctioned, but he's not saying by who, when or any other detail. I tell him it's also stolen and where from. Suddenly he knows nothing about it and directs me to ask Jeanie.

I identify a further eight pieces of stolen property as being bought by him on his own admission. He is now tying himself in knots and digging himself deeper and deeper. Why? Because he is on a seven year prison licence for a past offence of handling stolen goods.

Remember that 99% of the stolen property recovered was situated on land that Martin O'Connor supposedly rented. Only 1% was outside of it, but it contained thousands of pounds of garden furniture that was loaded up onto the back of some beautifully restored old trucks.

I ask him what he knows about this property and tell him I know it was stolen just before the warrant was executed. Panicking he gives a reason why his fingerprints might be on the stolen property. On and on he went, blaming his wife and anyone else he could point the finger at. Sat by his side was his solicitor who began to shake his head. The game was up.

At this point there is still a massive amount of work to do, but we now have some concrete evidence. The CPS reviewing lawyer advised us that a financial investigation into the suspects assets now needed to be commenced. This would involve examining the bank accounts of the workers to see if they had laundered any monies through them. We are talking about local people, some of whom were vulnerable, who may well have been forced into such money laundering criminality by the suspects.

When I thought back to the first interview; I likened it to a rugby scrum. If they had pushed us to our back line much further, we wouldn't have been in play. The second time we met them, we took some of that ground back and now it was them who were on their back line. We just needed a last push to get them over it.

By this time, there is just Mark and I dealing with the case. Lancashire provided us with some assistance, but there is still a lot of work to do. No other force will give us the resources to conduct a financial investigation into the suspects assets so in the end it took an instruction from a senior CPS lawyer to advise them they had to support and commence this side of the investigation.

It took another 18 to 24 months to conclude the financial investigation where hundreds of thousands of pounds were found in one worker's bank account that had been set up by Fred. Around this time, West Yorkshire wanted to wash their hands of the job. This caused a big rift between West Yorkshire and Lancashire who now felt we had left them holding the baby. They rightly argued that Mark and I had done sterling work. Mark was ready to retire, but they wanted me to stay on the case to ensure continuity with the investigation.

I was the officer who knew the job inside out, and I admit after becoming entrenched in the investigation, I wanted to see it through to the end. I had loved working on the case and wanted to finish my career on a high.

I couldn't understand why West Yorkshire insisted I be taken off the case and have to go back to Carr Gate. I'm reflecting on all of the high profile media coverage the investigation initially got and the victims who had lost their cars and vans, their livelihoods affected. We had done a good job, but I know when it really comes down to it no one appears to give a damn.

Mark and I had worked tirelessly for a year and for what? We had thrown everything we had at it. Against all the odds we had delivered a strong case to CPS. I had even put together a full dossier to illustrate who everyone was, what evidence linked them to the plethora of stolen parts, down to the minute detail of each interview. What we had matched, what had proved to be false. I had left nothing out. I handed it to the Lancashire officer, a detective called Nathan, who was taking over.

Nathan and another officer did a superb job. When it finally got to Crown Court, the suspects faced our case and further offences because they had still been operating during the investigation period whilst on bail. The Met Police had a case against them where it had involved over a million pounds of stolen heavy plant machinery linked to a business venture Fred had an interest in.

In Court there were legal arguments going back and forth but by the third day the Judge has heard enough. He's obviously had time to go through the case files and summary of evidence, including the detailed dossier I had prepared. He got the barristers together in chambers. No one can say what was actually said, but I would suspect it was along the lines of, 'this case can go on for weeks and weeks but if your clients are found guilty, I will throw the book at them.

With the severity of the crimes and the impact it had on innocent people, Fred could have been looking at 20 years. Begrudgingly, he and his wife pleaded guilty. The Judge ordered them to pay back £280,000 to their victims. Fred got six and a half years in jail and Jeanie fifteen months. Failure to pay back the monies would have gained them more jail time.

I had left the case with a heavy heart, but justice had been served. Nathan and his colleague had put the last bits of the jigsaw together, along with the financial investigators. It had been worth the hard work and long hours. The rugby match was over, and we'd pushed them over the line. The homework Fred had asked me to do had been completed.

After I was taken off the case it had a big impact on me as I desperately wanted to stay on it and finish the job I had started. After living and breathing the investigation day after day for nearly a year I had become engrained in it. I felt it was my destiny to remain and compete the investigation but that clearly wasn't happening. I also knew that the organisation was intending on returning me to Carr Gate.

So what? You may think. Remember this is the station where I had suffered bullying to the point of suffering a mental illness. I have also gone through the heartache with Sarah, and I am just pulling myself back up. I was bereft. I wasn't well enough, even now, to return to Carr Gate. I was actually scared to go back because I knew I could end up losing my job. Something would have given in me, and my long service would have been for nothing. I'm in 'No-man's-land' and I'm lost.

COLIN DIXON

Chapter 12 - No Man's Land

God promises to make something good out of the storms that bring devastation to your life.

To hear the words, 'You're going to Carr Gate,' sends shivers down my spine. Yet these were the words I was going to hear over and over, despite my protestations. Crime Division had taken me off the gypsy operation, which at that time was very disappointing. I had wanted to see it through. But to be told, there is only one alternative for you after 27 years of hard, dedicated police work, and that workplace is the one that almost broke you. I can't tell you how it feels. The knot tightens in the pit of your stomach. The memories flood back. I knew I couldn't do it.

It would be the straw that broke the camel's back for me. I can only describe it as a Tsunami I knew was coming. I had felt it rumbling for months and months and then, Whoosh; it hit me. It was devastating. I knew I wasn't mentally well, but I couldn't put a finger on what was wrong with me. It was something sitting in the caverns of my mind, waiting to be released. I was struggling to keep it in, hold it back, but felt I had to.

If I had been waiting for someone to show me some compassion, I would have been waiting for a long time. None was forthcoming. I knew if the organisation forced me back to Carr Gate, something would snap. Those that had caused me so much angst would have put something derogatory up on a wall, something would be said, or part of my work kit would have disappeared, and I would have lost the job I had given my all to. It was a step too far; I knew I had to do something. I had held it together for one simple reason, I was out of the way, working a single case and nowhere near Carr Gate.

I wasn't well enough to deal with this situation again. My short-term memory wasn't good. I had no desire to carry on. Anxiety was building up in me. I had lost my edge; I wasn't as sharp anymore, and I knew it. I was sleeping intermittently, waking up at all hours of the night and unable to get back to sleep. When I did eventually sleep, I woke up exhausted. I just didn't feel balanced. You know within yourself when you are not right, and I knew I wasn't.

I have used the boxing scenario before but here again; I was back in the ring, but now the ropes had been removed. I wasn't fit enough for another fight. This time it wasn't the trainer throwing in the towel. It was me. I had to get out of the ring or end up dead. My career and everything I thought I stood for gone. I think the thing that upset me most was the fact that the organisation could even think about sending me back to Carr Gate. Where was the duty of care? The responsibility for considering my welfare didn't seem important.

Looking back, I can see the mental anguish the place caused me was probably greater than the reality, but when you are in the situation, you cannot think beyond it. At home things weren't as balanced in our lives as they had been. I was anxious and worried, and nothing seemed to be as it should be. Mentally, I was going downhill. I can liken it to being in a snow globe where the picture is nice and calm and then, suddenly, something happens and it's shaken up so much you can't see beyond the bits of your life floating out of sync, all around you. The scene has lost its tranquillity, and a storm was raging.

I would have worked anywhere but Carr Gate, but someone, somewhere, decided I would not have this option. I was ordered to go back, full stop. The pressure and worry affected my already fragile mind. The more the pressure, the more vulnerable I was becoming.

All the time I had been in the force, I had rarely taken time off for illness and had an excellent sickness record. The realisation now was that counted for nothing. The hard work I had put into years doing a job I loved was null and void.

Carr Gate had effectively broken me, and during the gypsy job I had tried to repair myself, but when that was abruptly brought to an end it was enough to cause my mental health to shatter. I had previously given HR and supervision a full report of what I had gone through, but they didn't seem to acknowledge or understand my predicament. I had dared to tell a senior officer I couldn't go back, and it had now become a vendetta. They did not ask me to go and have an informal meeting or talk through the alternatives. All of which may have helped me and shown that someone cared, but it wasn't to be.

Who was I to speak to? Carr Gate supervision knew exactly how I felt, but it wasn't making a difference. Crime Division had spoken and removed me from the operation. I then received an email to inform me of the date I would return. It was linked to a confidential email I had previously sent to a supervisor, explaining the sensitive predicament I was in. That email had now been circulated to seven Sergeants, an Inspector and Chief Inspector who were all unauthorised to read it.

Someone had clearly forgotten to remove the long chain of emails, starting with the email from the supervisor in charge of the gypsy operation who had pointed out he was concerned for my mental wellbeing, going into some detail about my troubles, really quite personal things. Where do you go from that? It was clear they didn't know or care. Such a sensitive email just left for all to read. My life entered a dark place I never thought existed.

To continue would have caused irreparable damage and consequences. I had to take my only way out. I made an emergency appointment to see my GP, who then made an urgent referral to the Crisis Team. I was about to take the longest period of sick leave in my career. My past work history was to become obsolete. I was no longer capable of fully functioning as a police officer. I was embarrassed, humiliated, and felt as though I had lost all of my dignity.

The force doctor had read my GPs report and diagnosed me with clinical depression. I would be away from my job for the next seven and a half months. There are many types of depression, clinical depression is at the top of the tree. It is debilitating, and it affects every aspect of your life. There is no single cause, it can be anything from divorce, mental or physical abuse, situational causes, traumatic events, the list goes on. In 99% of cases though, the cause is too much stress over too long a period of time.

Over the last two years I had burnt my mind out with overthinking the stressful situations I had encountered. They say most people have periods of low moods, but it usually lasts a matter of days until the cause has dispersed. Feeling down is normal, we can't be at the top of our game all the time. With clinical depression, this isn't the case.

It puts you in a constant state of angst. Like most people I had no idea what the illness was until I suffered from it. In summary part of your mind has an area called the limbic system and in simple terms this area acts as a thermostat to control your mood, well-being, drive and almost every one of your essential day to day functions. For the vast majority of people this works perfectly throughout a lifetime, however, it's not indestructible and what can cause it to break is too much mental pressure over too long a period of time.

It has real symptoms and isn't a sign of weakness or something you can snap out of. Thinking, like I previously had, that you're too strong to suffer from it is like saying you're too strong to suffer from a common cold. Given the wrong life circumstances anybody can suffer from this very debilitating condition. You live, day to day, with the torment of your illness.

You lose interest in activities that used to give you pleasure. Your sleep becomes fractious, and you have no energy. You are tired for no real reason, feel worthless and guilty that you feel this way. Decision making becomes difficult and your concentration goes awry. Some people turn to alcohol or drugs to block out the nightmare. Your mind works against you, and you can't understand why.

Whilst I was off sick it felt surreal, almost as though I was lost in no man's land. During this time no one from work informed me about the support services available that the police could offer. I had to discover and arrange them myself, but I took advantage of every one of them. I had ten therapy sessions with the counselling services. I attended a two-week residential mindfulness course in Harrogate at the police convalescent home. I utilised the confidential listening service. I just wanted to get well again.

I felt the more people I could speak to, the more I could understand what was happening to me. I had completed 27 years of policing service and knew the strain of the last two years had taken a massive toll. Being too passionate about my work and taking too much on my shoulders all added to the damaged state of my mental health.

Now I could look back and take some time to think about where I had been and where I was now. It was time to stand down for a while to recover from the mental exhaustion I felt. Prior to diagnosis, I was uneasy about my mental state and even wondered if I was going into a form of madness. Some months earlier I had lost my brother to his own mental health battle and had been shocked at the very powerful and negative power it had over him.

Now a very dark force had entered my life and I couldn't stop it. My perception of who I thought I was, my purpose in the police, my home life, my social life. I questioned my very existence.

I received the odd kind message from colleagues, but they were few and far between. Not many people want to know when you are off sick with mental health issues. I understand they are busy with work and their own lives. When your illness is stress related, it can make it worse because a lot of people just don't know how to deal with it or what to say. My mind was working against me. I wondered if there was poison being spread about me in the workplace and people were fearful of contacting me.

In the police force, when you are off for over six months you go onto half pay. It's crippling and just adds to your stress. Sadly, your mortgage and bills don't half, they remain the same. After six months, I found myself fifty percent lighter in my salary. I tried to challenge the pay cut. I had been diagnosed with clinical depression and wrote a lengthy appeal to HR. I pointed out I had an excellent sickness record, had served the force well and been a front-line officer for 27 years. I highlighted there was evidence to show my illness had been arguably caused by the workplace at Carr Gate. The appeal was unsuccessful.

I thank God that I had a good support structure around me in my sister Carole, in my wife Sarah, my son Nathan, and a handful of other close friends and my dog Junior. I still had a home, and a roof over my head, but it made me think about the damaged officers who didn't have that. The ones you hear about who turn to drink and have been convicted of drink driving or some other offence. We were all thrown into 'No Man's Land' but I had a way out. Sadly, many don't.

Repeatedly, I had to relive and recount my story in various meetings with HR and the Federation representative. It was exhausting. I asked to be put into a temporary office role to get me back into work. It was enough for me to go to the meetings that were held at Carr Gate, but I had chosen times when I knew the team I had worked with were not on duty. I just wanted to get back to work again, somewhere away from there.

We eventually reached a gentleman's agreement. The organisation said they would get me back to work in a temporary position away from Carr Gate. They then said they would then look at other possible, more permanent positions I could subsequently move onto. A few weeks lapsed and I'm placed into the firearms and licensing team. I'm checking firearm certificates and in an office; Its tedious work but at least I'm back working. Now I have the opportunity to consider my next move.

Several weeks then pass by when an Inspector from headquarters where the firearms licensing team is based, begins to have weekly meetings with me. It's clear the focus wasn't my wellbeing, but he is acting as a go between with Carr Gate and myself. He's a nice enough man but here I am again, retelling my story, how draining it all is. I tell him I will do anything; I was happy to go onto the ANPR intelligence department or the call handling office. I knew this would have been difficult for me to adjust to, but I was prepared to do any other role than return to Carr Gate.

I'm told there are no positions in any other departments, Carr Gate appears to be my only option. I'm expected to go back and then put myself forward for roles that may or may not come up. I'm strongly protesting to him, but he is telling me I don't understand, and I will have to go back. Another tug of war begins the result of which is I deteriorate quickly.

Again, I am not sleeping; I am worried and anxious. The nightmare I dared to think was over wasn't. It was haunting me again, but this time furiously. There was no peace of mind for me. We played war games for several weeks. 'You are coming', 'I'm not coming'. On it went until I got back in touch with the Federation Representative.

He appeared to understand my situation and informs me he is concerned about my mental wellbeing. He can see from the way I am speaking and the things I am saying I am mentally unwell. He pre-empts this by telling me he has spoken to HR and police supervision about my condition but to no avail. Someone is adamant I am going to go back. I know what that will do to me, and I know in order to persevere my sanity I will go sick again before I returned there.

I knew by going off sick I would be on instant half pay, and it would financially cripple me. I was fighting internal and external battles and losing both. I knew if I went back and then put in a preference to leave, it could take a year or more before anything happened. I desperately wanted them to realise I wasn't being truculent; I was ill, and they didn't seem to understand that or didn't want to.

During this time, I sent an email to the Chief Constable highlighting the lack of support I had experienced during my seven months of sick leave. I asked if she would consider meeting with me. She replied saying that my words had greatly disturbed her and agreed to the meeting. I remember the day well. It was a lovely, sunny day in May. During my face-to-face meeting with her I outlined how the force did have access to excellent support services, however, in my time of need I had been left to find them myself. Many officers in similar circumstances perhaps wouldn't have been able to do this and in turn their mental health could easily have worsened.

My reason for seeing her had not been to complain about my situation, but to highlight the forces lack of contact and failure to inform me of the services available whilst I was ill. I suppose I was trying to point out some shortcomings because I knew this issue would not go away any time soon.

I offered my services to assist other officers going through what I was. I wanted to be part of the confidential listening service to show officers in similar positions, someone cared for them. Someone who had gone through what they were experiencing and knew what services were available and how to access them. I knew talking to someone like myself when I was at rock bottom would have helped me enormously. It would have made me realise I didn't need to feel ashamed of my illness and there was somebody who genuinely cared.

Now, I add, this was before the organisation had made it clear I would have to return to Carr Gate. At this time, I naively thought a different and safer position was being sought for me to move onto. She listens, showed interest but did nothing. She sadly never got back to me about any of the topics we discussed.

Some weeks later I was still in the same situation, only now I had been told there was no other posts in the whole of West Yorkshire Police I could go to other than Carr Gate. No place of safety. No respite to work out the last couple of years' service I had left. Surely, I had earned that, at least. The bottom line was the powers that be, who were digging in against me, wouldn't compromise. Carr Gate or nothing. Sadly, this caused my then fragile mental health to suffer, and I ended up on sick leave again.

The Federation Representative I had seen arranged a meeting with a solicitor. Once again, I relayed my story. She listened with compassion before telling me she would draft up a legal document for me to send to the Chief Constable. We also forwarded a copy of it to the senior officers who had been insisting I return to Carr Gate.

The letter was well written, detailed all I had gone through, and pointed out I had been diagnosed with a mental health illness. The document argued that the force hadn't made reasonable adjustments to help me. It also mentioned a breach of privacy concerning the email going out with my personal concerns attached. I take the following extract word for word from the letter.

'From a legal viewpoint I believe I have a mental impairment covered by the Equality Act of 2010. I believe that the force has a legal and positive duty to make adjustments and to look to remove any substantial disadvantages that arrive because of my disability and the force are failing in their duty to make reasonable adjustments for me. I suggest that during my present return to work the force has also failed in its duty of care, ensuring I have a safe working environment, this being safe both physically and in terms of my mental wellbeing.'

The thought of sending the letter saddened me. All I wanted to do was work in an environment where I could flourish and carry on with the job I had loved. I'm now really worried. Another three months and I would be on no pay and my career would be at an end. The financial connotations of leaving the force before my 30 years were served were massive. My pension would be affected, my lifestyle, everything. So not only would I have gone through the mental torment, without the support of my superiors, but now I was going to have to pay a sizeable amount of money for the privilege of going through this.

A short time after I had reluctantly sent the letter, I received a call from my Federation officer advising me that my case was going to be taken further. The matter was to be sent to the Federation supervisors to be authorised to take West Yorkshire Police to Court for breaching the Disability Act and for loss of earnings when all I had wanted to do was return to work. I felt some relief. Someone was listening, and I was going to get the help and support I so desperately needed.

Things then took a sinister turn. I received a further call to say the Federation supervision had not approved my case. They would no longer be supporting me. Why? I can never prove it, but what I can tell you is that the same senior officer I suspected of insisting I return to Carr Gate was also involved with the same Federation office. Call me sceptical but I'll leave you to make up your own mind.

Devastated is all I can say. Totally and utterly devastated. This was it, everything I had gone in a puff of smoke. I had no Court case to make some amends and returning to Carr Gate was out of the question. I found it hard to come to terms with how it had all got to this stage. We all have difficulties in our jobs, but they had thrown me into a pit which was deepening by the day.

We come into January, and I am fearing the worst. At the end of the month, I am going to be on no pay.

I was to be left completely in 'No Man's Land'. A once proud officer, stripped of absolutely everything. I had a constant feeling of emptiness in my stomach. They had ripped away my dignity in the most painful manner imaginable. I'm still a fairly young man and I'm on the scrapheap. I was back at the bottom, living a life of despair. It felt like they had taken my arms and legs away and left me with a damaged brain.

They say out of the darkness you find light. How and why, you don't know. I would like to think God took a hand.

'Life isn't just about darkness or light, rather it's about finding light within the darkness.' Landon Parham

I received a call. The call that saved my life, literally. In the depth of my darkness, I saw a light. Totally out of the blue, I was told there was an opportunity for me to start work at Halifax Police Station if I wanted to. It was a daunting prospect. The thought of going to a division I did not know. The IT had changed so much in the ten years I had been out of divisional policing. I was not only out of touch, but I also didn't know how I would cope.

All the things I had joined the force for we're now different. The civilian staff who previously did all of the complex work on Court files now had bigger workloads so some of that work now fell to officers to complete. I knew what this meant for many front-line officers; the self-initiated work had gone because there wasn't time now to do it. I felt vulnerable. I had no self-confidence, and I had unknowingly resigned myself to leaving the force.

There had been a massive increase in the number of reported incidents and the paperwork had become overwhelming. I thought back to the time when there had been a great camaraderie in the office. You had time to pass the day, share a joke or two, but now, there were hundreds of emails, reports, and calls to deal with. I envisaged being locked away on a computer, concentrating on a screen with little time to bond with others.

When I started all those years back, you learned the dynamics of the job and had time to develop the skills you needed. It was a slower pace. We had case files you could see, understand, and touch. You knew what was in it and what reports you had to write. When it's all on a screen and you don't physically have it in your hand, it's different. Some older officers like me look at the internet and its components, and it's like walking in treacle.

Still, I was more than grateful to have another chance, another shot, to do the job. So, from telling myself it was over for me, and I was finished, I had faced enough of the dirty politics; I reminded myself of the officer's anonymous email I've quoted from before and the pain and bitterness he expresses.

I didn't want to be that officer. I had to give it a go and I would. I told myself my career couldn't end this way; I would feel forever embittered. It would have meant Carr Gate had not only damaged me but had also finished me. I would not let that happen.

I will not lie. When I went to Halifax to meet my new boss, my thoughts were that the interviewer would be another Inspector, part of the machinery going through the motions, and I wouldn't be of any use to him. In I walked and sat before me was an Inspector called Paul Harkin, and during the time I was with him; he taught me the power of kindness.

He listened to me, empathised with me and halfway through the meeting he talked about Brian Clough, who has been an inspiration to me. He tells me he isn't interested in what I haven't got; he is interested in what I still have. I feel an immediate and overwhelming relief. Inspector Harkin asks me to join his team. The words meant so much. He tells me I will be okay. I'm not sure I will be, but I'm going to try my best for this man. He had given me hope.

I couldn't have been happier leaving his office. I was still frightened I wouldn't be able to do the work. I didn't know if I would cope with the IT. What I mean by that is I would be one of those veterans struggling to learn an alternative way of operating alongside tec savvy new recruits, I would feel quite embarrassed by my lack of skills and looked at differently by younger colleagues.

I had the street knowledge and, once confident again, I knew I could be one of the best self-generators of arrests there was, but the hours it would take me to input data in a system that was almost alien to me; would slow me down. Internally, I foresaw a division between young and old I'd already seen in the latter years of my career. I thought back to when basic computer systems first came in and remember thinking how they were, a good thing to have. They were simple to use and saved all the old typewriter, three-layer paperwork. It wasn't the case now.

I know my negative mental state is at work again, bringing doubt to a positive opportunity. I also know I have spoken to a man who isn't disguising himself as a confident who is really an enemy. Inspector Harkin isn't just another member of the organisation setting me up to shoot me down. Some of the faith I had lost in the force and in myself had reappeared in a matter of hours. A spark of life had come back into me. There was a possibility for me. No more Carr Gate tactics, no more deceit. He gave me hope and that raised me considerably.

Sarah and I were talking about things now where I had blocked her out of my problems before. She supported me in not going back to Carr Gate, irrespective of the consequences. She had gone through the same pain as I had with the thought of taking the force to Court. Remember, she is also a serving police officer. We both knew I hadn't wanted to take my employers to Court. I'd even got to where I didn't want the officers at Carr Gate punishing. They knew and will still know what they did, and I didn't want to carry it with me into retirement.

I had a growing faith in God, I had read Stephen Hawking's perspectives on the world, but I also read the work of scientists who held differing opinions to his. I did what police officers do; I investigated all aspects of faith and concluded there was something or at least I felt there was something beyond our human realm. It prepared me to search for it.

Inspector Harkin mentioning Brian Clough had given me a lot to think about. He had no idea the man he was talking about was someone I had great admiration for, yet it was the Inspector who brought him into the conversation. I had no desire now for revenge. I wanted to get back to work and prove to myself and to Inspector Harkin that I could still do the job.

In the words of Brian Clough, it isn't over with unless you want it to be. He was speaking to a player who had given up the same as I had almost given up, but now I knew I had a fresh chance, and I was going to put my all into it.

Chapter 13 - The Last Roll of The Dice

'You save your own soul by saving someone else's body'

I was at the weakest I had ever been as a police officer when I started working at Halifax. The role was taking me back to front line policing, one of the hardest roles any officer will do. It requires both physical and mental strength, and I had to question whether I was asking too much of myself. I likened it to being asked to run a marathon with two broken legs, only that you couldn't see that mine were broken. Inside I was damaged, but externally nothing was showing. I knew, however; it was my last throw of the dice, so I had to remove all doubt from my mind and get on with the job. Inspector Harkin had told me he didn't expect miracles from me, and I had to remember that.

Putting a uniform back on after 2 years felt so alien to me. I remember being in the locker room and putting my stab vest on and thinking this feels so very strange. It was the first time I had ever felt such an emotion in 28 years. I had to remind myself that Inspector Harkin didn't see me as damaged, but only as an experienced officer who would bring that experience to his team. His words had been motivational. He saw in me what I wasn't seeing in myself.

I hadn't been in a front-line role at a division for the best part of ten years, so it was very daunting to me. I wasn't strong enough or ready for the role, but I had to give it my everything, not to do so would have meant my job, my salary, my house, all I had worked for. It would have greatly financially affected Sarah and I for the rest of our lives.

So, in January 2018, I was on a neighbourhood policing team, (NPT), a role I had previously enjoyed in the past at City and Holbeck. It began slowly. I was trying to find my feet and get up to speed. New computer systems and thousands of emails missed since before I went off sick. So, as well as the return to front line policing, I was having to catch up with systems when I should have been slowing down in my career.

My lack of confidence was playing a major part, and I didn't know how I would feel back on the streets. One aspect of mental health is that you cannot see it. To anyone else I am an officer of the law, full stop. The NPT team shared an office with the response officers, and I could hear the furiousness of the radio with calls being received on a regular basis. The sheer numbers were overwhelming. On numerous occasions I could hear 999 calls being received with no officers available to attend them, it was unbelievable and nothing remotely like when I had joined the Force.

I know things change, but this was like chalk and cheese. The changes were immense. Mobile phones meant crimes were being reported more easily, drugs and their supply were on the increase as were internet crimes that included frauds and harassment on social media sites. Fewer police officers were on the beat due to financial cutbacks. When I had joined the average length of service on a response shift was 7 years, now it was 18 months.

Another difference was that people seemed angrier now than ever before. Domestic abuse and hate incident reports were on the increase along with everything across the board which had put a much greater demand on a now battered and beleaguered service. This is what I was jumping back into, and I didn't know how or if I would cope.

Once I had a physic reading, many years back. The gypsy woman had told me I would have a good career. It would be one I would enjoy and be passionate about but as I got to the end, I would feel I had climbed a mountain and as I neared the top, I would struggle but she also said I would reach the top and get down again safely. It's something I never forgot and coincidence or not, here I was desperately struggling to get up my mountain.

I thought back to my career. Other than the storm at Carr Gate, I knew it had been extremely fulfilling. I had reached the pinnacle of my game. I had a vast experience of policing, gained an immense amount of knowledge and, although slightly scared, was now raring to get back into it. It's amazing how many wild and wonderful thoughts go through your mind when you are unsure of yourself.

Observing the furore of IT and the intensity of the file preparation now required was alarming. I didn't know anyone at Halifax, so I didn't know who I could turn to for help. Who do you ask? Everyone is working their socks off already. I didn't have any backers, and I dreaded having to go cap in hand and reveal I didn't know what I was doing. So, not only was I worried about going outside, back onto the streets, I was anxious about the paperwork every cop has to do on the inside. My negative thinking was in overdrive.

I felt I was in a dense forest, and I didn't know which way to turn to get out. One path led to paperwork; the other path led to the streets. I felt lost and alone. I was initially doing four hours a day and trying to return to full time hours. I was aware of what the other officers must have been thinking. 'Why is he here?' they would ask themselves. I was still feeling embarrassed that I had suffered a mental health illness, although it's unlikely they would have known any of that.

I recall one day driving to work and on the way; I was listening to the radio; it was about a man whose wife had passed away in her 40s, and he was giving his testimony. A part of it I will never forget. He expressed his heartbreak at losing his wife and with losing her, he lost all hope. Everything he had was broken and he went downhill.

Then, one day, he had woken to think, 'What if?' What if tomorrow will be slightly better than today? He realised he still had two beautiful children that he had lost sight of. His message was to never give up on hope no matter how hopeless the situation is. The situation may appear hopeless, but his message was you are not.

It resonated with me immediately. Here was a man who had gone through arguably a lot worse than me, yet his talk somehow seemed to be aimed at me. He had picked up on where I now was. I understood the message. It was as if he was talking directly to me. I too had given up on hope. I was telling myself I could no longer do the job, and it was causing me fear. It was a light bulb moment for me.

I was an officer with 28 years' policing service and experience. They had decorated me with nine commendations, and I knew I had to shake myself up and change the way I was looking at things. I had to have faith in myself again, literally. That's when I started to look at what I had, rather than what I thought I hadn't.

Now at the time there was quite a big issue within Halifax Town centre with gangs of youths, 13 to 17 years of age. They were causing mayhem, from antisocial behaviour to assaulting adults who had dared to challenge their behaviour. It would be a good project for me to get my teeth in.

I researched who the ringleaders were, what crimes had been committed, by whom and which officers were dealing with them. I soon realised that no one officer was gripping the problem, the numerous offences weren't being pulled together and dealt with as one investigation. One suspect could have committed twenty crimes, but these were all allocated to a different officer, depending on who was working and when they were reported. The severity of the situation hadn't been fully realised.

I went to Peace Hall, an historic area of the town that is very popular with visitors. I had been allocated a crime where the elderly victim, 70 years of age and whom was a volunteer, showed visitors around the attractions. One day a group of the usual suspects had been swearing loudly. All the man had asked of them was to stop swearing in front of the visitors. He had asked politely, but for his trouble they had gone to the topflight of the stairs and, whilst he was talking to his visitors, one of the youths leaned over the balcony and spat on him. The spittle had gone behind his glasses and into his eye because of the angle he was spat at. A defenceless old man humiliated.

When I looked at the offending history of the lad who was the suspect, he had a list of seven current crimes against him, all allocated to different officers. I asked supervision to have them all reallocated to myself so I could deal with them as one. I knew if they were handled separately that it could take many months to conclude.

At the time these suspects believed themselves to be untouchable with little or no consequences from the police and judicial system.

Dealing with all of the investigations as one would have a greater impact on the suspect. It would also save a lot of time and the victims may feel as though some sort of justice was being served timely. I knew if we could show the seriousness and the sheer number of offences that were being committed it would have more of an impact with the Magistrates. It would send a message to the suspects that we were serious about clamping down on their anti-social behaviour and crime spree.

The spitting suspect was 15 years old and didn't attend school. His mum was a single parent who couldn't cope with him. He was dependent on cannabis. Due to changes in the custody process going straight to arrest mode was no longer an option. Dependent on what the offence was we now had to "invite" suspects in for a voluntary attendance interview. I knocked on the lad's door and spoke to his mum and made an appointment for his interview the next day.

The next day comes and he does what I had expected, he doesn't show up. This then gives me the power to arrest him at my convenience and I went to his house, but he wasn't in. I searched the streets and a few hours later find him and much to his distain inform him he is under arrest for several offences including his assault on the elderly volunteer.

He's interviewed over a couple of hours due to the number of offences he needs to be questioned about. Many of his answers to my questions are "no reply" ones and by the time we are finished he's been in custody for several hours. He's charged and bailed with some of the offences I'm investigating.

It's at this point experience and a thorough understanding of the cases are invaluable. I speak to the custody Sergeant and advise him I'm wanting to put bail conditions on the suspect, and I notice he raises his eyebrows at this suggestion.

I explain whilst I appreciate that the suspect is a juvenile, he's committed some serious offences and has a history of reoffending. The Sergeant agrees and we put conditions on the suspect not to enter Halifax town centre whilst he's on bail. The next day he breaches those conditions and I instantly go to look for him starting at his home address.

He's not in again but I explain to his mum that if they attend the police station tomorrow morning he will be arrested and put before the local Magistrates Court, thus avoiding a lengthy stay in custody. The next day comes and again he doesn't show up, so as

I'm on an afternoon shift, I scour the streets until I find him and arrest him for breaching his bail conditions.

By the time he's booked into custody there is no longer a Court open to hear his case, so again I explain to the custody Sergeant why he has been arrested as opposed to less intrusive options. For the first time this resulted in him remaining in police custody overnight until the Magistrates Court opened the following morning.

This is a fifteen-year-old lad who would comply with nothing. The next day, he went to Court, and it sent a loud message out to his other gang members to say we were getting tough. No more tickling the back of their necks. They were about to see what the law could do.

He didn't get a prison sentence, but we didn't expect that. What he did get was four months strict bail conditions that he knew, if he breached, would be enforced with vigour. Not being able to visit the town with his gang was a very difficult pill for him to swallow. I replicated this process with some of the other offenders in his gang. This helped me realise that I did still have it.

I had all the skills and tenacity I needed to fight crime effectively. By this time, I had made a couple of work friends.

One officer, Joe, a lovely guy, helped me considerably with the IT systems and in return I passed on my policing knowledge to him. My belief was returning, and I was feeling like I needed to put something back into the community before I retired. I got my opportunity when my wife Sarah, and her colleague, had been to a school in Mirfield and got the opportunity to listen to a guest speaker who was about to give one of four talks he did that day to the pupils at the school.

They had no idea who the man was or what his story was until they listened to him, but they were both in awe by the end of his talk. The man was called Paul Hannaford. It turned out that at one time; he had been so addicted to drugs that he nearly died. His story is horrific, and I will tell you more about it in chapter 15.

I listened intently to what Sarah was telling me, and I lit up. I thought 'wow, who is this man? I sent him a message on his website, and he contacted me back. I asked how much he charged for his visits, and would he consider coming to Halifax if I could get the funding? I then went to Inspector Harkin and told him about Paul and asked if we could fund him. Understandably, he raised his eyebrows. We were talking about a quite a lot of money, but I knew we could also do a lot of good.

A few weeks later, a restructuring of the NPT teams took place. The wheels turn all the time, and the bosses were assessing how we were going to do business in the future. During the meeting, Inspector Harkin revealed he had about £17000 left of POCA (proceeds of crime assets) money to be used for projects to help in the fight against crime. After the meeting ended, I was waiting in his office, repeating my request for some funding. I convinced him we couldn't lose. Here we had money seized from criminals, going to a once prolific criminal, to help stop young people from becoming tomorrow's criminals.

I got the rubber stamp to book Paul Hannaford for two days. Oh, my goodness, what an emotive story he had to tell. He made me look at myself and realise that I had been for a walk in the park compared to what he had gone through and overcome. When I was on a drug team, I had never seen a heroin addict walk away from their addiction and remain clean. I'm not saying some addicts didn't get clean, but if they did, I didn't witness it. To get off and stay off heroin has to be one of the hardest things in the world to do. His courage filled me with admiration.

Without him being aware of it, Paul Hannaford had made me take a good hard look at myself. If he could do what he was doing, what could I do? He made me feel empowered in a different way. It wasn't about ego or even me; it was about trying to get the best I could out of my last years of my service. I owed it to the force and to myself. This guy could help steer young people, bombarded with offers of cheap drugs at every turn, to say no.

I had been at Halifax several months by this time and was feeling mentally well again. I was in a positive environment, had officers who were supportive, and things were looking good. I had been involved in some worthy arrests and operations. I could see I was climbing out of the pit I had been in. I was regaining my strength. It had tested me to the hilt.

I had looked over the edge of the abyss and somehow pulled myself back. I had a good work partner in Joe and once again; I felt the wind was in my sails and once again enjoying going to work.

Looking back to starting at Halifax, I can now see how Inspector Harkin had been my rock. We are still good friends today and have often talked about the day we first met. He recalls me walking into his office. He sensed I was full of fear, thinking it was a set-up to be rid of me. Inspector Harkin knew I was having problems and was returning to work from a long period of sickness. He also knew how keen I was to move away from Carr Gate. He saw that as a positive start.

Inspector Harkin told me he saw my willingness, knew my attributes, and wanted to give me an insight into what he was trying to achieve at Halifax. I laugh, looking back, because he reminded me how quickly it had all been arranged. I had been in his office within a day of the invite. I didn't know at the time that he had looked into my background, talked to people, and found out about my service record, down to my commendations. There was nothing the man didn't know about me when I walked into his office that fateful day, more importantly, he was fully aware of my issues but took the view that everyone has problems at some time or other, so he was willing to give me a try.

He describes doing a bit of jousting with me at the start of the interview, but he was well aware that sitting before him was a man who had been broken by the job, but prior to this had been a first-class police officer for twenty seven years. He will tell you he knew I was still struggling. He even mentioned the slight tremor I had and how uneasy I was. It's ironic, but he noticed all the things good cops look for in criminals when we are dealing with them. Are they nervous? Why should they be nervous? What are they hiding?

It was a good thing he knew about my issues; he had realised quickly; I was suffering. It's strange how you rarely get to know how someone viewed you during an interview, but discussing it later with him, some things he saw in me, surprised me. He recognised I was being defensive and although I was trying my utmost to come across well; he knew my confidence was very low.

Enter Brian Clough. I have told you the story of our Brian Clough conversation but it's so amusing that both of us see this as the breakthrough point in the interview. We viewed the focus of the discussion differently; however, Inspector Harkin recalls Brian Clough as taking on a team of players written off and nursing them back to health. He probably saw me as written off by many and himself as Brian Clough whose "write offs" became a team of worthy players winning the European Cup.

Inspector Harkin hadn't made my background the barrier I was making it. I know reservations had been voiced by his Chief Inspector who was concerned they weren't getting someone at their best, but he had fought for me. What I didn't know until we spoke about things later was, he had got all of his Sergeants in, one by one, explained who I was, who they were dealing with and the way he wanted things to be managed. Apparently, they, like the Inspector, had considered the fact that I was willing to give it a go was worthy of their support, and that is what I received from them.

The fact that I was prepared to travel and take on the role showed them I had guts, and Paul said they liked that. It touched me when he told me he had made his supervisors aware they were not getting a polished product, but with work, someone who would become an integral part of the team. Inspector Harkin had gone as far as making sure I wasn't over challenged initially by giving me a beat in Skircoat in Halifax. It was an area where professional people lived, and they wanted solutions and a Police Officer contact to discuss any damage or antisocial behaviour taking place in their community.

When Inspector Harkin told me I fitted the bill, I smiled. Had he known what was going on inside of me, he may have thought differently. Thankfully, what he saw was someone who knew how to deal with people, someone professional and with the experience to overcome the difficulties of residents who wanted and expected a great deal from officers. A younger less experienced officer may have struggled with that expectation.

I am pleased to say I lived up to his expectations and beyond. He will say that I did a lot more than he envisaged. I had started off in Skircoat doing what I needed to do on a part-time basis, but quickly got involved in investigative work. Inspector Harkin saw me arresting and bringing people in again, even though he says I was rusty at first. I soon got into my stride.

I was always previously known for being thorough in my work. I earned my place on the team and my colleagues recognised my expertise. One of my proudest moments was when Inspector Harkin told me my work was exceptional, and he knew I was giving it my all. He knew I felt a need to pay him back for the faith he showed in me. He once advised me not to do too much as on many occasions I would do my shift, work some overtime and be back the next morning. I reassured him I could now see the light at the end of the tunnel and as long as I was being backed; I felt safe and strong again.

I know that within a five-month period of being at Halifax; I was a different person. I could smile again. My confidence was back. I never asked the Inspector to, but every few days we had a catch up chat to check I was okay. After experiencing so much insincerity from past supervisors I knew Inspector Harkin was genuine. I found myself telling him about my life. I felt my colleagues respected me and the need I had to prove myself had diminished.

My work didn't just involve dealing with criminals, I also worked with various partner agencies to deal with issues as a whole. That, in itself, was building me back up. Inspector Harkin told me from my starting to finishing at Halifax was like night and day. As our friendship developed, he saw me as being upbeat, thankful for my life and proud that I had overcome the part that could have easily destroyed me. He had never judged me and had seen me at my lowest ebb and later, at my best. I will be eternally grateful to him.

As my confidence returned, I delved back into the drugs world and learnt again, after twenty years, how to swear a drugs warrant and get it issued at Magistrates Court. These investigations weren't asked of me. I had taken it upon myself to develop pieces of drugs related intelligence and ended up obtaining over ten drugs' warrants.

I also utilised the force's new police interceptor team, a team of officers just like I had been when I was on the regional roads' crime team. They could stop vehicles that would no doubt fail to stop for ourselves. We were often being given vehicle registration numbers from members of the public that were involved in persistent drug dealing. After many hours of research, I put together a package of the most prevalent ones and this was fed into a briefing I would hold with the interceptors' team. On several occasions they arrested suspected drug dealers and seized their vehicles.

There was one time when Inspector Harkin showed immense faith in me. He was also a Police Federation representative and was dealing with a female officer who was going through some trauma because of what she had witnessed at work. He was helping to support her and asked me to be involved in a meeting with her. I could give her an insight into some of my issues and reassure her that it was possible to overcome anything with the right support. I like to think I helped her, but I know it was also cathartic for me.

There was a time we received a report about some heavy plant machinery being stolen from the Bradford area which had ended up in Halifax. The victim later sighted the stolen property and reported its location to us, but we couldn't get there in time before it disappeared again. Now the victim was angry and cursing at Inspector Harkin down the phone. Then, his MP became involved, and it soon reached our Chief Superintendent's desk as a complaint.

Inspector Harkin knew he had to sort it out quickly and asked me to take on the job. I had previously worked on cross border teams, so he knew I had the experience to deal with it. I utilised ANPR intelligence, linked three other unconnected thefts to this one and ended up arresting people, left, right and centre. I was opening up investigative avenues all over the country. The inquiry was growing legs and had reached the point where Inspector Harkin had to tell me to rein it in.

A real momentous time was when the Chief Superintendent heard about the work I was doing and the community issues I had been dealing with. He called a meeting with Inspector Harkin, a Sergeant and me. Normally being summoned to the boss's office can result in receiving a reprimand, but what he had invited us to turned out to be an afternoon of tea and biscuits.

All three of us were sitting in his office, waiting to find out what the meeting was about, when he simply said, 'thank you for the work you are doing in this division'. He didn't have to do that; he didn't have to say anything. It was a real morale booster. He then surprised us all by talking about the things which had happened to him, and I remember having an emotional conversation with him. I wasn't alone with my issues. It happened to others, irrespective of rank. It meant a lot to me, as it did for my supervision, for taking a chance on me.

As time passed, the number of calls being received became constant. The pace of policing was getting faster and faster, and the NPT were constantly back filling the gaps. When no one on response was available to go to an incident, we were being asked to deal with it.

Your own jobs had to be left, which I can understand, but by now they had diagnosed me as a diabetic and I was charging around like a twenty-year-old. It was taking its toll on me.

Sadly, Inspector Harkin retired at Christmas time in 2018, and he was greatly missed. My record of successes was mounting. The youths in Halifax town centre had calmed down and were no longer openly abusing people. They had learned that there were consequences to their actions, and I was going to make sure they received them in full. I was off the ropes and doing what I knew I could do. I was thriving again.

There was one time I recall when I had been up since 4.30am, rushed a bit of breakfast, and got to work. I was executing a drugs search warrant. At 6am we smashed the front door of the property in and several hours later was just finishing processing the prisoner involved in the job. It's now 2.30pm, and I was just about to sit down for a meal when a 999 call came through.

Now, I've been on active duty for eight and a half hours without a meal break and I needed to eat something urgently to keep my blood sugar levels stable. My collar number is then shouted over the radio, and I am ordered to go on the call. I get in the van and end up being involved in a minor collision because of my low sugar levels.

I'm nearly at the end of my thirty years and I'm getting concerned about my health. The constant round of assaults on my body, which numbered nearly 300 in 30 years. An assault can be anything from a push or shove to a violent attack.

One night towards the end of a long shift I was asked by my colleague if I minded if he called for some food from a local takeaway. I'm sat in the van answering a phone call when he returns and tells me a man is lurking in the shadows near a cash point and he has verbally abused him.

We decide to speak to the male and find out what is happening. He then tells me to fuck off repeatedly. Enough is enough. He's arrested and I manage to get one handcuff on him but then he goes absolutely berserk. He's yanking the cuffs I am holding onto with such force he damages the tendons in my arm. It doesn't stop until I get my incapacitant spray out and manage to use it on him.

He's going wild, wanting to cause serious injury to me. He's full of vile comments and I can feel the determination in him with the violent struggle we are now entwined in. I knew if he had been in possession of a knife, he would have had no hesitation using it on me, but now he had done enough to ensure I was carrying an injury. I manage to eventually subdue him.

We then discover he had a long history of criminality, and his MO is waiting in the dark for unsuspecting people to come out of the pub and use the nearby cash point where he had previously robbed them.

He's only in his 20s but his list of offences is lengthy. One is an alleged charge of rape against a nine-year-old boy, another a robbery and then we learn that he himself had been a victim of rape at an early age and whilst it doesn't justify his criminality it makes you realise what trauma he suffered as a child.

I worked on with this injury but then we got a call a few weeks later involving a fifteen year-old boy and his dad who had settled in the country from Iraq. The boy hadn't adjusted to the move well, and his dad couldn't control him anymore. We get to the house; the boy is at the top of the stairs with a knife in his hand. He has slashed part of his face to the extent where the skin on the side of his cheek is flapping and he's covered with blood.

I'm at the bottom of the stairs trying to reason with him when he throws a shoe at me, a sign of disrespect where he comes from. I'm glad it's the shoe and not the large knife he has. He then throws the knife on the floor, and we cautiously go upstairs and manage to handcuff him.

Next minute he is going crazy and spits at me directly into my eyes. The dad is looking so embarrassed, and I felt nothing but pity for how they had come to this. As a result of this injury, I had to have a blood test and wait several weeks to establish if I had caught HIV or any other transferable disease. The violent and dangerous situations I was being sent to appeared to be on the increase.

I was coming to the end of my service and sensed I was going to get past the finishing post. I also realised I was now in a race where I was struggling to keep up with the pace of today's policing.

In my last week of service, the first shift started at 7am and didn't see me finish until 11pm. We had arrested a career criminal who had been in possession of a knife. Disturbingly, he had eleven previous arrests for the same offence and hadn't long been released from prison. We had received a call from a terrified female who had seen the male brandishing a knife in a park.

My partner and I approached him with my incapacitant spray already drawn. I was leaving nothing to chance. I remember the look he gave me after I had searched him, found the knife and arrested him. They say the eyes are the window to the soul and this man's eyes were displaying evil. He needed to be remanded and it was a very long, (17 hours), but worthwhile shift. That was in July, and I was scheduled to retire in October.

I returned to work at 7am the next day and received a lovely report from another teams Sergeant praising my work ethos. It gave me a boost even though I was tired. To have my dedication recognised meant a great deal to me. Then, on the penultimate day of that week I worked, my supervision asked me to go to a call involving a stolen motorcycle which had been seen in a suspect's garden by the mum of the victim whose bike it was.

Prior to visiting the location where the bike had last been seen, I talked to mum and advised her the bike may well now have disappeared, and we may not recover it, but I would still go the house. Due to the demand of calls again on that day no other police colleagues were available to attend the incident with me. I had researched the suspects address and based on the intelligence I knew it wouldn't be safe to be attending this address alone.

I attended with Ben, a PCSO. I knocked on the door and it's answered by a young woman. Before I can explain why we are there a man is screaming from an upstairs bedroom, verbally abusing us for attending the address. He then hurtles down the stairs and it's at that point that I activate my body worn camera and ask Ben to do the same with his.

The man is full of hatred and contempt as I tell him why we are at the address. He's stood there in underpants, smelling of cannabis. He swears at us, says there's no stolen bikes here and to fuck off, he then grabs the woman back into the house and slams the door into our faces. Based on what we had been advised by the victim I looked around the garden for any signs of the stolen motorcycle.

Seeing this he runs out of the door and confronts me in the garden whilst still in his underwear, screaming and issuing threats. Enough is enough, I get hold of him to arrest him for a breach of the peace but during the violent struggle to handcuff him I end up pulling my shoulder again and I'm in agony but with Bens help manage to overpower him and arrest him.

After he was booked into custody, I could see that he has several impending investigations for dishonesty related offences including burglary.

It took a few hours to prepare a handover package for the suspect as by the time I had obtained a detailed statement from the motorcycle theft victim, along with an injury on duty, use of force form and an arrest statement, I ended up working past my 3am finish time. Just prior to 6am I had put all of the cases together in order for another officer to interview the suspect that morning.

Before finishing work, I sent an email to my supervision, a new acting Sergeant, to advise him of the situation and that I had been injured. I also indicated to him that I would be commencing work that same day a little later in order to accommodate an 11 hour break between shifts. I had worked another 13 hour shift.

I went home and was in agony with my shoulder injury but managed to eventually get to sleep at about 9am but only for a few hours. Exhausted I set off for work in the afternoon, common sense told me I should have rung in sick, but it was my last working day of the week and I wanted to see it through.

When I got to work, I immediately sensed all wasn't well. After an hour the acting Sergeant asks me to go to his office and the door is closed. I am questioned about why I had to work overtime and who had authorised it. I inform him that those details were on my email I had sent him, and I had worked the extra hours for time off only, not for payment. I reassured him that I really had wanted to finish my shift at 3am, not 6am.

I'm then advised that the suspect has made a complaint and questioned as to why my body camera was turned off halfway through the arrest. At that time, I had no idea it had been switched off. Thankfully, my colleague's camera was on and when we look back at the footage it's clear that during the struggle the suspect grabs hold of my body armour and camera and in doing so has inadvertently switched it off.

I had been asked lots of questions concerning my integrity, but the most important question was never asked. Are you ok after being assaulted for a third time in as many months?

That was my last day at work as the pain in my shoulder was by now excruciating and was only numbed with strong painkillers. I knew I couldn't continue to physically operate safely and to have done so would have been reckless. A subsequent visit to A and E for a scan on my injured shoulder revealed that I had torn tendons and now had degenerate damage. This injury, along with a major operation to remove my gall bladder, saw my last three months of policing being spent on sick leave. Not how I ever envisaged my career ending.

I ended up going to the police convalescent home in Scotland at the end of September for heat treatment on my shoulder. The doctor makes it clear to me that if I don't take care of myself and my shoulder that I risked suffering a long term injury. I was still weak from my operation and just couldn't take the risk. I didn't want to retire like this, no goodbyes or proudly going to work on my last planned day of thirty years, but under the circumstances I had no alternative.

Some months later I did arrange an event to celebrate my retirement. I went back through all of my years on the force and invited special people to commemorate my thirty years with. Forty plus people attended. We had a beautiful evening, colleagues who meant something to me surrounded me. A few days after the event, I received my certificate of long service through the post. The frame the award was in smashed. It said it all. That could have been the end, but I turned a negative into a positive and took my certificate to a framing shop and had it restored. Like myself it had been broken but was now repaired.

Some months later I had a meeting with the Chief Superintendent at Halifax. It lasted a good hour, during which he apologised for the way I had been treated in my latter few years by West Yorkshire Police. He also thanked me for my service, and all the poor and disappointing experiences dissolved into nothing. I thought only of the many good times I had enjoyed. Before I left his office, he said something I will never forget, "Colin, don't ever let others dim your light, shine brightly in your retirement" I walked away feeling totally content.

I had said goodbye in my own way, and I could now retire in peace.

Chapter 14 - Politics and Policing

'Politicians are interested in the next election, police officers are interested in the next generation'

An anonymous Police officer wrote, 'We are like robots. We turn up to work, we answer the calls, and we fill in ALL of the paperwork, most of which is completely unnecessary and duplicated simply to cover ourselves.'

He is referring to the external politics and the Government guidelines tying our hands at every turn. Every organisation is political but usually the people involved in those politics are at the top of the chain. Those at the bottom simply get on with doing their jobs. I was no different and didn't feel directly affected by them. Yes, I knew what we were doing internally, differed greatly to what the senior management team were portraying externally, but like most police officers, I obeyed my orders and did what was asked of me.

Government cuts, shortages of officers and resources had made it impossible to do the job we should have been doing, so we did the best we could. We were often using plasters to cover gaping wounds. If I'd have been in charge, would I have done the same? I can't say, no one honestly can until you are in that position. So, politics to me was something you had to put up with. Most officers did a good job even with the restrictions placed on us, but the face of policing shown to the public was nothing like the reality we knew it to be as officers.

'I'm done with the duplicitous liars and twisters of the truth in Parliament, who have destroyed policing in order to further their own careers. I'm done with the charlatans and snake oil salesmen and women who spread their bile, whose acid eats away at society and it's values and future.'

These are strong words from another anonymous police officer, but they represent the feelings of many others. The problem with Government officials' involvement with policing is they never ask the front line officers what they think and more importantly act on their recommendations. More often than not, they are pandering to the public and looking at balancing budgets.

What I knew, but at that time, hadn't experienced, is that the internal politics can be just as destructive as the external ones. If you challenged the internal politics, there would be repercussions. Supervision would see you as a maverick or troublemaker. Yes, I'd had my moments, like everyone, but I was never work shy and I produced good results. I had passion and loved doing the job.

I took my Sergeant's exam but didn't get promoted. It was in three stages. The first part was studying legislation and involved four areas: traffic, crime, general police duties and law. It involved reading hundreds of pages from the four books. You then had a written exam and had to get 75% to pass. It took me five years to pass the first part but then you have to pass part two, based on practical scenarios. They give you a briefing or an issue to resolve. So, in 1999, and after seven years of study, I was qualified to the rank of Sergeant.

Promotion isn't instant though; you then have to take a third part which requires a member of the senior management team to support you. It was then I realised the real vengeance of politics. I had previously raised issues such as chronic short staffing levels and had challenged authority at times but now I would pay the price. I couldn't get the support or backers to get me through this part.

So, ask yourself, is it about looking at the qualities an officer has and the job they have done, NO! Is it about passing an exam, and I'd done that. Passing those exams wasn't enough though, you were then required to pass the 'boys' club' test. It was a simple case of if you were in the know and hadn't rocked the boat, you would get supported and if not, you wouldn't.

By this time, I had met Sarah, and it was then I really experienced how internal politics worked. They had moved Sarah to another station, but I refused to be moved. Although I didn't want to, I was happy to move shifts, but I didn't see how my relationship with Sarah could warrant being forced to move stations. An Inspector overseeing the situation had a meeting with me and advised me in no uncertain terms that I would be moving as I had caused a lot of upset to others within the organisation.

I already knew that, but the Inspector couldn't see that it had also upset me. I had paid a price in losing my dog, access to my son whom I loved dearly, and my home. My life was in total turmoil. I didn't feel as though I could cope with any more changes. I almost pleaded with him to understand. I so badly needed to keep some normality and that was the station where I worked, I didn't want that to disappear. I was happy to move shifts, but nothing I said resonated with him.

Sarah and I were certainly not the first couple to meet and fall in love whilst being in another relationship, and I'm positive we will not be the last. Do you forbid love? What happens if it takes place in a regular firm, a solicitor's office or factory? You can't move those people involved around when there is nowhere to move them to. I was being made to feel like a criminal for falling in love with Sarah.

I ended up taking sick leave whilst the situation remained as it was. The Police Federation then became involved, and meetings were held with the Inspector. One of which ended almost as soon as I had sat down when I realised it was not about my welfare at all. It wasn't about resolving problems; it was about creating them for me.

The conversation centred around what police housing benefit I was receiving and the fact that I was not living at my home anymore. The inference being that they were looking at stopping this allowance. Disgusted that this was the starting point of the meeting I clarified that the legislation for being eligible for this allowance was that I had a mortgage. Although I was no longer living at my home, my housing allowance still paid towards that mortgage, and this was all that was required to maintain the benefit.

I turned to the Federation representative and told him we were leaving the meeting. He got up, and we walked out. Three months on and the organisation conceded I could stay at the same station but move to another shift. The exact same compromise that I had offered to accommodate this situation three months earlier.

Politics were still at play. Some of the senior officers on the new shift I was now on challenged my integrity. They micromanaged me every step of the way. Questioned decisions I made, but it was all done very subtly. My daring to challenge being moved had placed a bullet in the guns chamber, now it was only a matter of time before the trigger was pulled. Politics veiled and at their worse. I knew this situation wouldn't get better, so I made the move to City & Holbeck as outlined in chapter 7. A move they couldn't interfere with or stop.

I'd been at the new station for around five months when the opportunity for the third part of the Sergeant's exam came back up. I approached my Inspector, but he rightly said he couldn't support me because of the shortness of time I had worked for him, it would have to come from Wakefield. I knew what the outcome of that would be, of course, and I was correct. The Inspector at Wakefield wrote a damning statement of my last weeks' working there. That was in total contrast, I add to the excellent yearly review my Sergeant had given me prior to leaving Wakefield division.

The only saving grace I had was that I had taken the option prior to leaving Wakefield to talk to the divisions Chief Superintendent. This was the same man who had previously awarded me with three commendations. He had thanked me for the time I had served at Wakefield. We both knew the last year hadn't been a good one for me and I was being forced to leave, but I thanked him for the four good years I had served there. We shook hands, and I left.

I appealed the decision through him, and for the first time I had ever known, a senior officer overruled another senior officer and pointed out my good service. He had also contacted my new Chief Superintendent, who had told him my work results at my new station were excellent. Had I not gone to meet him and thank him, I know I couldn't have approached him with the appeal with any prospect of success. Politics at the fore again, but he was kind enough to see through them. This was a year since I had met Sarah, but the backlash was like a heavy chain I was still carrying around my neck.

I never became a Sergeant, although they had signed me off to take the third stage. I wasn't supported, so I never got the heads up on anything and I never got a promotion. How do I feel about that now? Strangely, things have a way of working out. When I originally applied five years before, Sergeants still went out on the streets with regular officers, but by the 2000s it had changed so I know I wouldn't have enjoyed been office bound, sat behind a computer most of the time. At that point, I let it go. I was happy where I was and going to make the best of it.

I knew the politics, like the bullying, discreet as they were, would not change. It still exists today and always will. I was one of those characters who needed a little more handling, but does that make me a bad police officer? Are we saying people who tell it as it is, are going to be micromanaged out of the Force? Are they going to be denied promotion? Such people are also the ones who can make the very best officers.

I'm sure I was seen as a bit of a renegade by some of the senior management, and they felt the need to exert their power and control over me. In my opinion this is how they handle a lot of personnel; they make sure they know their place in the scheme of things. We are in a disciplined service, so I understand that ethos, however, this rarely works as you go back up the ranks. I have to mention here that several people who made my life difficult when I met Sarah were having relationships with other officers. Two in particular, Sergeants, had an identical situation to the one Sarah and I were in, but unlike us, they were allowed to carry on in their roles, working alongside each other.

Internal politics happen everywhere and one thing I realised is you ignore them at your peril. They can be manipulative, vicious and career wrecking. It's not enough we often face the hatred of the public, but we also face the hatred of some of our colleagues. That isn't to say there weren't some good bosses and colleagues because there were, but often, they remained on the side-lines whilst you are in the middle of the scrum. When you become aware that promotion to the next rank is dependent as much on keeping your head down as on your abilities, what do you do? For most you keep your head down.

The blue wall of silence has been written about and questioned as to its existence. Wikipedia describes it as: The formal code amongst police officers not to report other officers' errors or wrong doings. In the US, it's also known as the blue badge code and written about openly. Less so in this country. Breaking the code is said to lead to severe repercussions, is there any wonder then that discreet bullying and victimisation goes on often unchecked.

Politics play a pivotal role in the promotion process. Any sign of non-compliance, being too vocal or vocal at all, can end any chance you have of moving up the ranks. I've mentioned before the time I stood and talked about issues affecting policing at a police conference, only to be told by an Inspector that he was amazed I hadn't been sacked. I guess it made me think of the George Orwell quote, "In an age of universal deceit, telling the truth is a revolutionary act".

Eventually, you recognise you have to put up with the deception and be the elephant in the room, but if you tried doing something with the elephant, you wouldn't get very far. You toe the line, or you suffer the consequences, the residue of which is not just that which is visible but also the invisible. The damaging effects political play has on your mental wellbeing. I paid the price for falling in love with a colleague and paid for it for a long time. Was I naïve not to heed the politics? Perhaps I was.

The following quote is from a Greek Statesman called Pericles, written in 495 - 429 BC and sums it up.

'Just because you do not take an interest in politics doesn't mean politics won't take an interest in you'

Internal politics has played its part in the bullying and harassment of colleagues throughout history. More often than not, for reasons I have described, it goes on under the radar, but most police officers will tell you of its existence. Those officers who dare to write about it remain anonymous for fear of reprisals.

I end this chapter with another quote from yet another anonymous officer.

'I'm done with senior officers who will jump on any bandwagon, throw any officer under a bus for doing their job, do anything at all to get that next rank and more power. I'm done with them pretending to be cops when they are just politicians in uniform.'

That quote sums it up for me. I was an officer who refused to go back to Carr Gate. The place where I had been bullied and broken to the point of despair. In my time of need I was asking for help to return to a safe working environment.

Nothing more, nothing less. I wasn't trying to be insubordinate; I was fighting for my sanity. I couldn't go back. To do so would have mentally damaged me beyond repair. Politics, however, once again showed no compassion.

OUT OF THE STORM - A COP'S JOURNEY

Chapter 15 - From Darkness to Light

'The two most important days in your life are the day you were born and the day you found out why'

So here I am, retired from the police force which had been my life for 30 years. I have so many wonderful memories as well as some very bad ones, but I've come through it. I've learned a lot; my recollections are vivid, and I find it a privilege to be in a place where I can openly and honestly share my experiences with you. Why did I decide to write this book you may ask?

The answer is partly because of the unique experiences I had during those 30 years that I can share with you. My main reason though was to hopefully show you that no matter how hopeless a situation may be, that you as an individual are most definitely not hopeless. Never give up on hope, it's often at its darkest just before dawn.

Would I be in the position I am now in if things hadn't happened as they did? Would I have reflected on who I was as a person? Would I have found faith had my life not showed me deep darkness? I don't believe I would.

I can look at things in two ways. Firstly, I can ask why I had to suffer as I did, why after 26 years of dedicated service, did the end of my career in the police become so difficult. Focusing on this could have resulted in me being very bitter and angry and would have eclipsed the wonderful years I had doing a job I loved.

Secondly, I can concentrate on the positives during my career which I did. This empowered me to be thankful that I had now found a renewed hope and faith and with that total contentment. I remember reading a quote from a book that resonated with me.

"You are not a victim; you have control over your reactions. You do have a choice"

In my darkest days I thought of my grandfather who had fought in World War 1. He served for 18 months in the trenches in France in a hell most of us can fortunately not imagine. Shot and left for dead in no mans' land he suffered from pneumonia and a shrapnel injury, he was rescued just before death took him. I was blessed to meet him before he passed away in 1975. My mum told me that he never once complained of the hardships he experienced before or after the war. I'd like to think that I have inherited some of the resilience that he possessed to get him through those horrendous times.

Once I had regained my mental wellbeing, I made the choice to reflect on my 30 years of policing in a positive light. The hard times at Carr Gate showed me the power of forgiveness and where true strength lies.

The way some of the senior management team had dealt with me showed that I now had to focus on myself and my future rather than dwelling on the past and any injustices I felt I had suffered. The hard times brought me into contact with people that have influenced my life for the better and my journey of faith has been strengthened through it.

I do sit and cast my mind back to the hotel where I had my retirement do. Here I said my goodbyes to the colleagues who had meant so much to me. I thanked each of them individually for the part they had played in my career. These were the people who really mattered. I described my 30 years as a marathon and said every one of them had handed me a cup of water when I needed it and had given me inspiration to strive for better things. I will always appreciate them and in my own way, I gained closure.

I remembered the words of Dickie Whitehead, the Chief Superintendent who had the meeting with me shortly after I had retired. The praise he gave me as well as the apology on behalf of West Yorkshire Police. He acknowledged the poor treatment I had received towards the end of my career. All words that meant so much, but none so much as his last words to me.

'Colin, don't ever let others dim your light, shine brightly in your retirement'. If you read this Dickie, I want to say thank you to you for believing in me.

I was now learning that I could turn many of the previous negative situations I had experienced into positive ones. I know my faith has guided me through and it's made me realise, more than ever, life is not about the things I do for myself, but more about what I do for others. I now see myself as a branch on my tree of faith, no more, no less, and all I am expected to do is to develop and grow. Knowing that brings me inner peace and contentment of the like I had never experienced before.

Over the days and weeks after leaving the force, I did a lot of soul searching and I knew I was starting to find a peace I had never experienced during my time with the police. My life became much more settled. Sarah and I had a new understanding, and we became a constant support to one another. We had both been on our journey's. I had hit rock bottom, but I had survived.

Sarah had seen the difference in me and wanted to be part of the new journey with me. She wanted peace and unity as much as I did. Together we decided we would walk the same path and we do to this still today. Our once devastated foundations had been rebuilt, this time with God mixed in and we are stronger than ever before. We are both empowered more than we have ever been, and we both see that as a blessing.

It still left the question, what was I going to do now after retirement. I was relatively young at 53 and certainly not ready for pipe and slippers. It was then I was approached about working with male perpetrators of domestic violence. It was a colleague who contacted me to explain there was a job vacancy as a facilitator should I be interested in the role. At first, I wasn't sure. I had just left behind all of the angst of dealing with violent offenders. Did I really want to work with them again?

The pressure I would place myself under by taking on a commitment like this was something I needed to consider. I couldn't agree to give the role a go and then back out, but to say no when I knew I had the experience and skills needed went against the grain. I had previously dealt with the type of men I would be teaching on the programme, but now I wouldn't be arresting them, I would be helping them or trying to help them discover a new path in their lives.

As a police officer, I hadn't really stopped to consider the reasons why men abused their partners. To be honest I didn't have the time or inclination to understand them. I had a job to do, and that was to stop the violence as it was occurring and remove them from the situation. To take on this new role I would have to look at domestic violence from the offender's viewpoint so I could understand how to try and help them. It didn't mean I would ever condone them being abusive, I wouldn't, but perhaps they were lost in their own anger and trauma and knew no different.

'Domestic violence and abuse are defined as any incident of controlling, coercive or threatening behaviour, violence or abuse between those aged 16 or over who are or have been intimate partners or family members, regardless of their gender or sexuality'.

I knew I would have a lot to learn. As an officer of the law, I had many dealings with the physical side of domestic abuse, but not in the other areas of psychological, sexual, financial and emotional abuse. It would mean a new challenge, but I knew I wanted to help the victims of such abuse.

Two months after I had left the force, I started the job, and through it enhanced not only my skills of empathy and understanding but also the need to get perpetrators to be accountable for their own actions. Domestic abusers, more often than not, do not recognise the impact their actions have on others. I gain a lot of satisfaction when I can see in their eyes that the penny has eventually dropped.

The course itself is not something the men can dip in and out of. They have to do 17 very intensive weeks, each session lasting two and a half hours each week. If they successfully pass the course and there have been no further incidents of domestic abuse, they can return to family Court and apply to see their children. It's not guaranteed but it is a real incentive for them to attend and pass the course.

I remember one man who came on a course, he really didn't want to participate or take an honest look at himself and his abusive behaviour. He was purely attending to get access to his children via what he thought would be an easy route. I knew that was the case with some of the men on the course but to see the way they changed as the weeks went on gave me real hope.

This particular man, however, showed no signs of changing, then came the day I told him he had a choice. He either took the course seriously and participated or he walked out of the door. I said to him 'but before you walk out of the door, let us send your children out first'. His eyes said everything. He sat back down and began looking at himself differently. His 'I shouldn't be here' attitude changed.

Running the course is not just one sided. I learn a lot about myself from each session. It often makes me think of my parents' relationship during which there was a lot of control on my father's part. No physical violence but certainly control, resulting from a strict 1800s style upbringing by his own father. The role has helped me to see the issues in my own upbringing and there effect on me. There are always reasons for what happens in life if we open our eyes to them. It justifies nothing, but it creates understanding.

I use my childhood example of the relationship between my parents. It surprised some men to recognise abuse is a control mechanism which turns positive partnerships into negative ones and starves both parties of love and affection. It's a powerful message delivered to the group.

It's similar to the message Paul Hannaford gives to the children and young people he shares his experiences with.

So, who is Paul Hannaford, and why do I admire him? I have explained earlier in the book how when I was on a drugs team, I never saw an addict get clean and remain free from heroin until I met Paul Hannaford.

COLIN DIXON

Twice he almost died from his drug abuse. He wrecked his body so much; his legs will never heal. His mind was a mess, and, in his drug addled days, he stole £2000 pounds' worth of goods each day to pay for his £500 a day addiction. Yet, by a miracle, he got himself clean and has remained so for the past twelve years. Now, he spends his days giving his powerful testimony to thousands of school children in the hope that they won't make the same mistakes he made.

Why am I including Paul in my book? We were on two opposite sides of the fence. He, the criminal shoplifter, and drug addict, me the hard-working cop, so what do we have in common. We both have faith and hope; we have learned to forgive, and we have changed our paths in life. We are now good friends and both work for the benefit of others. We give back to society and in doing so; we are learning to heal from within. We were on separate journeys but have both gone through our own hells. I don't profess mine was the hell Paul lived his for 20 plus years. it wasn't, but now we are on similar journeys. We both had positive outcomes, but it could have been so very different.

Before we met, Paul's life had been a revolving circle of prison cells, drug hovels, and hours of oblivion under the influence of the strong drugs ruling his life. Why he started using drugs he puts down to many things. Naivety, being the first. He had no idea what a few spliffs of weed could lead to. His parents had broken up. He needed to belong to the in-crowd and in weed he found the comfort he was looking for. The drug changed his state of consciousness and he blocked out what was hurting him.

To Paul, being stoned removed the focus on anything else in his life. He realised it had become a problem for him when he would wake up and need a joint, knowing he had put one out before bed. He was only 14 years old and already dependent. So, some kid saying to him it won't happen to them doesn't wash with Paul, he has lived it and probably said the same when he started.

It was the same with me on my courses with the perpetrators who feel one or two pushes or slaps doesn't constitute domestic abuse. They Initially minimise their actions and behaviour and in doing so fail to realise the impact such behaviour has on their victims.

Like me, Paul turned to alcohol in his times of darkness. I had been the same. We had both vowed never to drink again, but of course that was only until the next one. To admit you like the feeling of being out of it, whether drugs or alcohol, is hard but until you can recognise it, you can't get off the slide into darkness you are on. I was more fortunate than Paul and realised the effect drinking was having on me early enough to jump off that slide. It took Paul many more years to realise.

Drug overdoses, hospitalisation, near death calls and a run through the minefield of various drugs would happen before Paul took the courageous step to go cold turkey.

I had realised a long time before the devastation that heroin brought to people's lives, so it came as no surprise when he pointed it out as the most harmful drug in the world. Just seven years after taking that first drag of weed, he was taking his first heroin hit and knew immediately he was lost. The drug had got hold of him. He quickly turned from an 18 stone, fit young man, clean and conscious of his appearance, to wearing the same underwear for days on end, sharing needles and losing all sense of dignity and reality.

Paul had lost all respect for himself. He had lost all consideration for anyone or anything other than for heroin and the numbing effect it had on him. For very different reasons, I had also lost my self-respect and dignity and the life I had known in the force. To differing extents, both Paul and I had lost a sense of ourselves and of our families.

What did we have in common? Life itself, we both took a leap of faith. We both understood that there was a lot more to life than what we had. For Paul, a split second of faith saved his life. For me, it made me realise the way I was to move forward was entirely down to my choice. No excuses. No one else.

Paul now spends his time talking about his experiences with children, some of whom could well go down the same path. In the same way, I am helping men understand the path of abusive behaviour they have chosen is their choice and they can choose to change. Neither of us judge and that means we are more effective in the work we do. I don't judge what background the perpetrators on the course are from in the same way Paul doesn't judge about the circumstances the young people he talks to are in.

I remember going for lunch with Paul and thinking what a strange combination, a long serving cop and an ex-drug addict. We were as different as chalk and cheese, but we were both on the same hymn sheet. I would like to think we share a mutual respect for each other. We have a very honest relationship; Paul knows the pain I have suffered, and I know the hell he came through. We have a shared understanding of life and how easily it can get messed up. Our experiences are different, but the positive outcomes are the same. Our lives are now concerned with forgiveness and helping others.

Which leads me to the end of this chapter with the following quote first made over 2000 years ago.

"For now, three things remain, faith hope and love. But the greatest of these being love" Corinthians 13:13.

COLIN DIXON

Chapter 16 - Reflections in Time

'Retirement is a blank piece of paper, a time to shape your life as you want it'

If I said to you, I was a totally different man today than the one whom in 2015 was just going into the biggest storm of his life, I wouldn't be wrong. I also never imagined I'd finish my time off in the police on sick leave, but life rarely turns out as you planned. My vision for many of those 30 years was to end on high octane, adrenalin rush filled jobs, still catching criminals. The work I had thrived on. The sort of jobs that start out as nothing but turn into something big. My ideal type of policing, the type I specialised in and was driven by.

30 years on, I thought about the prophetic message from the gypsy fortune teller. She had foretold my future correctly. I had climbed the mountain and yes, with my darkest days both in and out of the police, I had fallen into a quick decent but there were other factors that I knew had affected me. The injuries I had sustained on the job, in battles with criminals who didn't know when to give up. Two near fatal car accidents because of sheer tiredness and back breaking shifts. The repetitive damage to my shoulder which was one of three serious injuries I sustained within the last four months of my service, culminating in me going to the Police Scottish convalescent home to receive medical treatments.

Castlebrae is one of the several police treatment centres that are located all around the country. It is in a place called Auchterarder and is set in six acres of alluring, peaceful grounds close to Perth. Spending time in such a beautiful setting helped to heal me mentally, which I needed as much as the physical healing. I felt a sense of release from the pressure I had carried with me for 30 years. It was a surreal feeling, the reality that I would soon no longer be a police officer.

I knew the torn tendons in my shoulder would take time to heal, as long as six months in most cases and twelve months if the rotary cuff has been injured, so I was under no illusion the healing process in Scotland was going to be a quick fix. It wasn't, but I knew somehow the only way I could move forward now was to put my faith in God and to keep checking myself every time I looked backwards in a negative way. As I have said earlier, to forgive is to forget. A quote I like regarding forgiveness says:

'Forgiving people who have hurt you is your gift to them. Forgetting people who have hurt you is your gift to you. Always forgive your enemies, nothing annoys them so much. You have to forgive, to forget and forget to feel again'.

It took me a long time to really believe in forgiveness. It is a choice, an act of will, but often it doesn't happen overnight. As I started to look around me, I could see I had such a good life. Sarah and I were bonded together again, stronger than ever. I had a facilitator's job where I was giving back by helping others. I had my dog walking business, small as it was. I had a good pension and a peace I hadn't felt in a very long time. The combination gave me a good work life balance. Dog walking is simple, healthy and rewarding in the same way that being a course facilitator, helping domestic abusers to change, taught me so much.

I don't think anyone would tell you with any honesty; they don't spend a lot of time reminiscing once they retire, especially if, like me, they had been in the same occupation for 30 years.

You must remember that the wear and tear on the body and mind of a police officer is not the normal wear and tear of a person in a less confrontational career. As you get older and are repeatedly assaulted, you feel the physical wear and tear more. The fact was that I had been on the front line much longer than the average officer. Most officers move into specialist jobs after a few years, and I fully understand why. I served the majority of my service on this front line, and I know that it cost me with my physical health later in life. I reflected on the number of injuries, just short of 300, that I had received. Some were serious, some not so serious, but over time they slowly wear your body down. Injuries that leave you with bad knees, arthritic hands and aching backs.

I think the mental toll on a police officer is often worse than the physical injuries. It changes your perception of life; your view becomes distorted by the negativity surrounding you. You are either dealing with the victims of crime and feeling their pain or the offenders that have caused that pain. Offenders that are involved in a range of criminality that includes child criminal exploitation where children as young as 10 are exploited to sell drugs and store weapons. The drug dealers who control these gangs now appear to thrive with impunity.

Murders increasing year after year, usually as a result of gangs fighting over turf for the rights to deal drugs as their biggest fear now is not the police but other rival gangs. Weak borders and the ineffective enforcement of illegal immigration. A complete and total lack of respect for law and order, people in certain sections of society who actively challenge and goad officers. Waiting for something controversial to be said or done and then filming their interactions and circulating them on the internet and social media sites.

Wracking your brain day upon day, asking yourself, "how have past and present governments allowed crime and disorder to become almost uncontrolled in many places" does nothing for you mentally. The problem is, of course, when you are actively policing day after day you see the very worst of society that is normally invisible to others. It's very easy to get a distorted view and become too consumed by this environment.

Now I think it is what it is. It saddens me but I've realised I cannot change what it is, but I fortunately don't have to be exposed to it anymore. I'm no longer in a position where I am constantly dealing with the victims or perpetrators of crime. I'm no longer seeing the hate in criminals' eyes or the terror they put their victims through. I'm not holding the hand of some mother as I inform her that her son has died.

Maybe I was too dedicated and thought and cared too much about things. If I had to give any new officer advice today it would be, 'Don't get too serious about things, take it as it comes'. I would ask them to realise what they can and cannot change because however much you think you can do in the job; you soon learn you are a tiny cog in a very big wheel, and you will not change the world however much you give of yourself.

I was full of passion; I got too emotionally involved and when I became mentally unwell and was at my weakest and needed help from the organisation there was no recognition of this. Despite this I look back at my policing career with great pride and fulfilment as the good and great times far outweighed the bad ones.

Today I live a simpler life. I take responsibilities for my actions, and I endeavour to see things in a positive light. Although I went through a very difficult time, I don't view myself as a victim, I'm most certainly not. I don't judge others and I don't expect them to judge me. My perception is now much more balanced, and I savour my life. I may drink the same wine but now savour it rather than swallowing it down.

The intensity that policing fills you with has now gone and I'm at total peace with that. We all choose the path we tread and mine is now full of hope and love, and I thank God for that. I am happy and at peace. I've unchained myself from the force and I feel the freedom of normality.

As I now come to the end of my story, humbler and less cynical than I have ever been, I can say openly I am not the gladiator I thought I was, but I am now the man I have fought to become. No longer do I view life through the lens of a black and white camera, now I see the full colour.

THE END

COLIN DIXON

MEET THE AUTHORS

Colin Dixon dedicated thirty years of his life to the Police Force as a front line officer. During that time, he saw death, destruction and the depths of evil that elements of the human race are capable of committing.

Colin was passionate about his work, receiving many police commendations for his outstanding performance as a police officer. Colin handled the most difficult of situations professionally and with compassion. What he didn't realise was that the greatest threat to his mental health was not an external job related one but sadly, one that was in the organisation he had devoted his life to.

What he experienced next was two years of hell that led him to the edge of a mental abyss he wasn't prepared for. Against all the odds Colin recovered but never forgot the mind destroying anguish he suffered at the hands of some of his trusted colleagues.

OUT OF THE STORM - A COP'S JOURNEY

In writing this book Colin hopes to show you, the reader, that no matter how hopeless a situation may appear, you are not hopeless and never will be. You can choose to be a victim, or you can recognise that you have choices. Colin's sole purpose in publishing his book is to provide an insight in the physical and mental impact that thirty years in policing can have on an individual.

'Out of the Storm' serves as an inspiration to others who may be going through their own personal storms and demonstrates how faith and forgiveness can empower you, giving you the strength, you need, to come out of the darkness into the light.

Patricia Sutcliffe is an author and life-writer who has two best sellers to her credit. An ex-university lecturer and experienced behaviourist, she achieved her first accolade as a writer when aged ten, winning a nationally run school competition. She turned to writing full-time, becoming a published fiction writer before moving into life-writing. Her first novel 'Tormented' received all 5 star awards.

Her enthusiasm for 'real' life story telling came from her study of forensic criminology and her love of the novels of Charles Dickens. She studied 'Advanced Life-Writing' at Oxford University and has a Degree in English plus a Master's in Strategic Decision Making.

As a ghost-writer and co-author, she dedicates herself to helping others who want to leave a legacy for their families but who lack the time or skill to do it for themselves. Her work and reviews can be found at www.patriciasutcliffeauthor.com